PENGUIN BUSINESS
JOB SEARCH SECRETS

Subir Verma is head, HR, at Tata Power DDL. A writer, speaker and start-up mentor, he is an engineer and postgraduate from Xavier Institute of Management, Bhubaneswar. In the twenty-four years of his professional career, he has worked in information technology, telecom, retail, financial and manufacturing sectors. He was previously head, HR Business, at Tata Power, director, HR, at Tata Communications, chief human resources officer at Augure, and general manager at Reliance Communications and Reliance Industries Limited.

Subir has been conferred with HR Leader of People's Choice by *Businessworld*, CHRO of the Year by World HR Forum, Best TA Person by *Hindustan Times* and Power of Idea Winner by the *Economic Times*.

He is on CII's Committee on Industrial Relations as well as the advisory board for Atal Innovation Committee (Nalanda) under the Startup India programme of the Government of India, and is an honorary academic adviser to many institutes, including Kalinga Institute of Industrial Technology School of Management and Poornima University.

Dr Sagarika Verma is a PhD and MBA in HR with over fifteen years of experience as an entrepreneur and in the corporate world in the area of human resources and consulting. She has been associated with ICICI, Indian Institute of Management Indore and Indian Institute of Technology Kharagpur, before she caught the entrepreneurial bug in 2002 and founded Idream Consultants and www.idreamjobs.com. In 2009, the organization was recognized as one of the top five companies in eastern India, and that same year, she moved on to new pursuits.

She has also been associated with UNDP, the National Association of Disabled's Enterprises and Indian Development Foundation (working towards leprosy elimination and TB control), and IIFT.

Sagarika has been featured in the *New Indian Express*, *Dainik Bhaskar*, the *Samaja* and on Doordarshan. A prolific trainer who has mentored professionals from over thirty companies, she was conferred with awards for the Best Learning Company and the Best Women Leader of the Year at the Future Leadership Summit.

ADVANCE PRAISE FOR THE BOOK

'Job searching can feel like an overwhelming and daunting task. Job descriptions have vague language and hidden meanings, and job sites feel like an endless amount of pages of jobs you didn't know existed. This book is an insightful and practical guide for finding the right job and nailing your application every step of the way. Read this book and find your dream job!'—Marshall Goldsmith, *New York Times* #1 bestselling author, *Triggers, Mojo,* and *What Got You Here Won't Get You There*

'Thousands of talented people struggle to land deserving jobs because of their lack of understanding of how the job market and the interview process works. The book therefore becomes extremely relevant—both for first time entrants to the job market and those who are looking to make a mid-career switch. I hope more and more people read the book so they can crack these job search secrets and achieve their true potential'—Amit Malik, CEO and managing director, Aviva Life Insurance Company India Ltd

'A methodical and step-by-step approach has made this book indispensable. This book will show the path not only to those who are starting their career but also mid- as well senior-level professionals'—C. Jayakumar, vice president and head, Corporate HR, Larsen & Toubro

'An outstanding work for the thousands of people who struggle with their search for the "right" job. Helping understand that right job, looking for it beyond the obvious, preparing oneself to secure it. An easy read, backed with some very practical tips to find a better job. The book is a must-read for any job seeker, today and tomorrow'—Prabir Jha, CEO, Prabir Jha People Advisory, ex-CHRO, Reliance Industries Limited, CIPLA, Tata Motors

'This is the most relevant book in our current times that helps you achieve your goal'—S.V. Nathan, partner and chief talent officer, Deloitte India

'Subir Verma and Sagarika S. Verma's book *Job Search Secrets* is a practical handbook for all those who are looking for the right job. The book is a labour of love, reflecting a professional depth which comes through years of hard work and practical experience. Choosing a career you love is the first step to the path of success to take forward your passion, but equally important is to secure the job you love. This book is a great tool to help you achieve that. I wish the authors every success and look forward to more books that help job aspirants and HR professionals alike'—Ratan Bhardwaj, chief editor, *Breaking News*, NDTV

'*Job Search Secrets* is a much-needed book in today's world of business, where there is a demand-supply gap of right talent. A book that outlines a practical approach and convenient methodology for a job search with insider tips and secrets is definitely worth a read for every job aspirant. The "start to end" approach on how to bag a job of your choice makes the book an interesting read for many job seekers. A commendable book'—Amit Das, director, human resources, Bennett, Coleman & Co. Ltd

'This book is a promise to help millions of job seekers through a systematic approach to find a job. The ubiquitous gap between the need for talent and the talent's need for jobs can be bridged by using the advice by the authors to job seekers. Lucidly written with easy-to-follow steps, this book is a must-read for Individuals looking to find jobs, better jobs, change jobs'—Neharika Vohra, professor, IIM Ahmedabad and vice chancellor, DSEU

'A must-read for all job aspirants, cutting across age and present job profile, this book aims to do what has not been done so far—put in place one composite ready reckoner for job seekers. The mix of theory and practice makes it a unique read'—Dilip Chenoy, secretary general, FICCI

'If you Google the topic "job search", you get 7.5 billion results in a second! That itself shows how important this subject is and that billions of people are seeking answers to the questions around job search, which is so important in one's life. With the pandemic, these questions have become even more important. This book will surely be a very useful guide for every job seeker and help them navigate their approach towards securing a job. A book with a lot of practical insights and tips, which make it even more helpful'—Prem Singh, president, Group HR, JK Group and honorary president, National HRD Network (North Zone)

Job Search Secrets is not just a good book, but it's a "necessary" book in today's competitive and challenging job environment. This book provides an insightful framework that offers practical tips and suggestions to be successful in this fast-changing job market'—Pradyumana Pandey, chief human resources officer, Mother Dairy

'This book is just wonderful and a must-read for all job seekers. This book will be an inspiration for young minds aspiring for corporate careers to reach greater heights in choosing a career, not just a job'—Sudhakar Balakrishnan, group CEO, FirstMeridian

'*Job Search Secrets* is a must-read for all job aspirants. In today's VUCA world and with the uncertainty in the job market, job aspirants need detailed guidance on "how to enter the business world" and their chosen "dream company". The book is very well written, understanding aspirations and challenges'—Prof. Sayalee Gankar, vice chancellor, D.Y. Patil University, Pune

'This book is path-breaking with treasures inside for all youth to find the right career choices and succeed. With its simple writing style, structured and fact-based approach, it is easy to follow and helpful'—Kavita Dasan, chief people officer, ABP Network

'This book is certainly going to be extremely helpful for millions of job seekers. The book is a result of hands-on experience in recruiting thousands of people over the years; it provides valuable lessons and insights to aspirants seeking enhancement of their career prospects. A must-read for all who are at the crossroads of their work-life!'—Aditya Mishra, CEO, CIEL HR Services

'Finally, we get a book that simplifies the overwhelming task of finding a job. What I have liked most about this book is the focus on finding the "right job" and not just any job. The authors have carefully put the professionals at the centre stage of job hunting and have equipped them with a methodology that is guaranteed to yield results. This book is destined to make millions of job seekers smile!'—Munish Kumar, chief executive officer, Quess Healthcare

'India has millions of qualified graduates but most are without a job. Companies have vacancies but not the talent. There needs to be a bridge which can prepare talent to be ready for what companies are looking for. *Job Search Secrets* provides just that. Short, practical and effective tips for all students and job aspirants to find jobs. Many secrets are revealed, and I recommend all to benefit from it'—Suresh Chandra Padhy, president and vice chancellor, Poornima University

'*Job Search Secrets* is full of real insights and is a practical guide that not only touches upon the art and science of getting the "right" job, but also how to remain happy in the job. This book will play a big role in equipping readers with the right approach, to land their dream jobs'—Tojo Jose, chief human resources officer, Muthoot FinCorp Ltd

'*Job Search Secrets*, written by Subir and Sagarika, acts as a career coach for students and job aspirants to find all the answers'—Nivedita Nanda, group chief human resources officer, Kaya Limited

'The biggest confusion for youngsters is "Which career is right for me?" and "How to get the job of my choice?". Students and job seekers experience many barriers to be gainfully or rightfully employed throughout their career. They need to know how to overcome these barriers with the right resources and support. *Job Search Secrets* is a tremendous, practical and much-needed work. They have mindfully compiled the different perspectives related to the challenges being faced by job seekers and how effectively and efficiently they can reshape their inner and hidden capabilities to address the challenges with the right information and guidance that is most suited to everyone. A wonderful book'—Anil Gaur, group chief people officer, Uniparts Group

'This book is bringing out pertinent points related to the current job market . . . a struggle between right talent and unemployment. Get the benefit by putting things into practice'—A.G. Rao, ex-group managing director, Manpower Group India, ex-executive president, TPT (Tata Teleservices)

'This book by Sagarika and Subir is about to fulfil people's dreams to get corporate jobs. The book creates practical and multiple bridges between talent and employers and helps you find jobs in the corporate sector'—Ashish Vidyarthi, national award-winning actor, founder, Avid Miners

'Who wouldn't want to read a book with a title *Job Search Secrets— Master the Art of Getting a Job*? It is structured in a way that readers will be able to understand the science behind the art. The book doesn't need a testimonial; if you read and implement it, you will see the results yourself'—Harjeet Khanduja, vice president, HR, Reliance Jio

'A book by experienced and accomplished human resource professionals which will change the lives of many people. An immensely valuable piece for all job aspirants and students'—Ashoke K. Maitra, founder and CEO, Sri Ramkrishna International Institute of Management, Mumbai

'This book truly reveals the secrets of success to cracking campus interviews, finding hidden jobs and the right people to get a job, building long-lasting networks, choosing the right career, managing virtual interviews, using job portals and social media, negotiating salaries and joining company. All with practical tips, tricks and free tools of each of the areas needed for a job search. A must-have book for all'—Prof. Hiresh S. Luhar, director, VIVA Institute of Management

JOB SEARCH SECRETS

Master the Art of Getting a Job

Subir Verma
Sagarika Verma

BUSINESS

An imprint of Penguin Random House

PENGUIN BUSINESS

USA | Canada | UK | Ireland | Australia
New Zealand | India | South Africa | China

Penguin Business is part of the Penguin Random House group of companies
whose addresses can be found at global.penguinrandomhouse.com

Published by Penguin Random House India Pvt. Ltd
4th Floor, Capital Tower 1, MG Road,
Gurugram 122 002, Haryana, India

Penguin
Random House
India

First published in Penguin Business by Penguin Random House India 2021

10 9 8 7 6 5 4 3 2

ISBN 9780143453079

Typeset in Adobe Garamond Pro by Manipal Technologies Limited, Manipal
Printed at Replika Press Pvt. Ltd, India

www.penguin.co.in

We could not have done this without the inspiration of our parents, late Shashi Kumar Verma and Anita Verma, and Umesh Chandra Sahu and late Gauri Bala Sahu. This book is a tribute to their teaching: 'Be good and do good, always. You are successful in the true sense only if you make others successful.'

To our daughter, Nehal Nitya, whose innocence and sensitivity towards others reminds us of that teaching whenever we lose track.

Contents

1. Choosing a Career That Will Make You
   Happy for Life   1

2. How to Select the Right Job and Company
   (and the People Who Can Get You the Job)   16

3. The Ways Companies Recruit
   (and the Best Options for You)   33

4. How to Best Use Job Portals and Job Aggregators   56

5. Professional Networking Sites or Job Portals   69

6. How to Make Attractive Profiles on LinkedIn to Get
   Discovered by Companies   89

7. How to Go about the Job Interview—
   Before, During and After   102

8. Cracking the Campus Interview   129

9. Things to Consider before Accepting a Job Offer   152

10. Be Unique; Get an Edge with a Video Résumé   166

11. Virtual Interviews Are the Future   176

12. Leaving a Job Gracefully   192

1

Choosing a Career That Will Make You Happy for Life

Searching for a job is always stressful. The majority of job seekers experience stress, nervousness, anxiety and tension during their search for a job, regardless of their work experience, their current compensation level or the industry of their choice. There will be many factors at play that are not in their control, such as a bad economy, hiring freezes, unexpected corporate mergers, buyouts, etc. However, one of the main reasons for stress during the search for a job is the candidate's lack of confidence, which comes from a lack of planning for the search and a lack of practice at it.

It is time to take a step back and really think about your own approach to this before cursing yourself or blaming your lack of success on the companies you are applying to. Even before you go out to apply, you must have your job search strategy ready. A well-planned approach will not only help take you through the process faster, and with better results, but will also make it less stressful.

The First Step

The first step is to decide what *you* really want to do.

Selecting a career based on what others are doing (or under peer and social pressure) may give you the desired results in the short term, but long-term success and self-fulfilment will always be missing. In India, many parents want to fulfil their dreams through their children. Parents usually advise their kids to become what they could not become themselves. It is also common to see parents asking their children to emulate the success of the children of their relatives or neighbours. Parents always want the best for their kids, and there is nothing wrong with this. However, when it comes to career advice, most parents have limited knowledge. For example, traditionally, the most popular career choice for a commerce student in India has been chartered accountancy; for a science student engineering and medicine; for the arts students the creative fields, management or the civil services. If you just copy others to make your parents happy, you will end up pressuring yourself unnecessarily. Such an approach to choosing a career can be disastrous, because what worked for others may not work for you. Always remember that a career choice that simply follows another's will not give you the excitement, happiness and passion to excel in the long term.

It is equally true that many of us choose our careers without much thought. In fact, many a time we simply accept whatever comes our way.

However, you should not blame yourself if you have chosen a career in this way. It is not your fault. As a young job aspirant, you had limited exposure, experience and knowledge of the options available.

What YOU Want is Important

There is no harm in being ambitious. However, if your aspirations are too broad or varied, it will be difficult to act; you will lack direction, and will not know where to focus your energy. Many job aspirants are confused as to how to choose a career for themselves. After all, their choice has long-term implications. Hence, your choice needs to be practical. It should not just be based on your current state of mind, the environment you are in or the desire of your parents.

What you really want to do in life is worth ruminating on.

A career should be selected on the basis of certain parameters, which will act as the foundation on which you will build it. Your entire career trajectory will be shaped by your one decision. Therefore, be extremely careful while choosing a career. In fact, it is highly recommended that before you actually start applying for jobs, you write down certain relevant details about yourself, your desires and needs, in a notebook, or save them in a document on your computer for future reference.

To decide on your long-term career options, you must consider the following:

- Your educational qualifications
- Your behavioural attributes

- Your SWOT (strengths, weaknesses, opportunities, threats) analysis
- Your interests, likes and dislikes

Here, we will use a real-life example to better understand how a career decision should be made.

Sunil is an MBA and a native of Khagaul, a small town near the state capital of Bihar, Patna. He has been an average student throughout school and college. He plays cricket and football during his free time and has lots of friends in his area. His father works with the Indian Railways and his mother is a homemaker. He has three siblings and lives in a joint family. After graduating, he has applied for all the jobs published in the newspapers and on job portals. He has sent out more than 200 applications but has still not found any success!

Every job aspirant is unique and therefore each needs to employ unique job search strategies. As we said earlier, what worked for someone else may not work for you. Here are some insights for Sunil to make a simple yet effective job search strategy for himself.

Sunil should first introspect, and write down these details about himself with regard to the four aspects mentioned below:

1. Educational Qualifications:

Companies give a lot of importance and attention to the educational qualifications section of the résumé of a fresher or a job aspirant with less than ten years of experience. This section should contain, in addition to your formal qualifications, the courses you have completed and the skills you have acquired. Start with your most recent educational degree, diploma or certification, along with the year of passing out, college name and examination scores. Please write your cumulative grade point average (CGPA) or marks (only if they are good and will create a good first impression). Don't forget that your résumé represents you, so write things that are true. If you have done any professional online course relevant to the job for which you are applying, you should certainly mention it in the profile.

We have seen many job aspirants with a postgraduate qualification in management and an engineering degree search for jobs on the basis of their previous qualification, which is engineering. They completely overlook their latest qualification—management—in this case. In his curriculum vitae (CV), Sunil should not only mention his graduate degree, but also the last two to three qualifications, courses or programmes that he has completed. This will increase the scope of his job search and the chances of his CV getting shortlisted. If Sunil has done a course in social media marketing, email marketing or public speaking, he should mention that too in the résumé. These are relevant qualifications and will create a positive impression about Sunil, showing him as a person who is proactive, takes the initiative and makes an extra effort to constantly learn.

You can see how important it is to mention all your relevant qualifications in your résumé. Apart from your main qualifications, all the short-term courses and the learnings and skills of the last five years must be mentioned. You may even go back to your school days and think of those special classes that taught you a skill relevant to the job you are applying for.

2. Behavioural Attributes:

Technical skills alone are not enough to be effective and successful. A marketing person who has knowledge of a product and its market will have little success if he or she does not have the interpersonal or negotiation skills to close deals. Most engineers or management graduates have similar domain knowledge; however, what differentiates one from another is their soft skills. While hard skills or domain knowledge is easier to acquire, mastering soft skills requires consistent effort and takes time. In an interview or at the workplace, soft skills decide the winner. Communication, presentation, creativity, problem solving, collaboration, adaptability, agility, positivity, ability to work under pressure, ability to take criticism positively and ability to influence others are some of the soft skills that you must mention in your CV and present well in your entire job search process.

Sunil should analyse his personality and list down all his behavioural attributes. While listing down his personality attributes, he should also take into consideration what others, including his family members, relatives and friends, think of him. It is important to consider the opinions of others, as most of the time one is either over-confident or overly self-critical. Hence, while writing down your behavioural attributes in your résumé, it is recommended to consider how your family and friends see you. Let this be a long list. Do not be judgemental about any of these things now. It is important to list down all that comes to your mind at this point in time.

Complete the personal table below:

Educational Qualifications	Behavioural Attributes
Write down your last two educational qualifications (example, graduation/MBA)	Make a list of what you think about yourself
Write down all the other certifications and skills you have acquired	Also list what your family and friends say about you

3. SWOT Analysis:

The SWOT analysis is one of the best analysis frameworks that job aspirants can use. This analysis helps them customize the best job search strategy for themselves. Sunil must use the SWOT analysis to devise an effective job search plan for himself. It will help him focus on his strengths, tackle his weaknesses, take advantage of the opportunities available to him and plan to eliminate possible threats. It will also help him unravel opportunities that may be hidden and unspotted. Just like Sunil, you must also use the SWOT analysis to create an effective job search plan for yourself.

You need to capture all your strengths, weaknesses, opportunities and threats. Decide on the goal you are writing the SWOT for, which, in this case, is the job for which you are applying. Remember, this exercise is about the self, and no other factors should be included in this section. In the strengths section, you should list all the strengths that you strongly feel you possess. It is a human tendency to be either too boastful or too critical of oneself at times. Therefore, if you are not able to think objectively about your own traits, recall what your friends and family tell you about your strengths. Go and ask them, if required. Again, let this section be as long as it gets, till you exhaust what you have to say. Do not be judgemental in selecting or rejecting any strength.

In the strengths section, you should list your qualifications, certifications, skills, experience, connections, achievements, projects, networks and personal attributes. Don't forget to mention what differentiates you from others; that is where you are better than others. Also, mention the resources and support systems you have.

The weaknesses section should have the tasks you try to avoid, your negative habits and fears as well as the personal traits that hold you back. It should also include the things you consider boring, your habits that people complain about, and the feedback people give you for your betterment, among others. In fact, in this section, you must include all the missing skills and traits that you think, if acquired, can help you achieve your goals faster.

Opportunities are all about a favourable external environment. These are also the factors that already exist, and if you are able to explore them better you can achieve your goal faster. In the opportunities section, you should also write down what unique technologies or skills you may have learnt, which could give you access to a more diverse set of jobs. In this section, you must also mention the people you know. These are the people who can help you find a job, whether in your industry or in another, should you wish to move to another industry.

Threats, like opportunities, are external factors that are already present; they may also appear in the future. These include inability to relocate for a job, personal traits (weaknesses), lack of job opportunities in your identified geography, the competition in your area of qualification or experience, etc. These factors prevent you from achieving your goal. For example, if, due to any reason, you are not able to move out of your current place of residence, then you should list it as a threat in your SWOT.

Let us understand this better with another example. Jyotishikha is a computer science engineer with five years of work experience as a software developer. She is happy with her job but does not love it. Whenever she gets the time, she learns digital marketing and does more and more online marketing work. She has also completed an online postgraduate diploma in management in social media marketing. She has always had an inclination towards marketing.

Here is her SWOT:

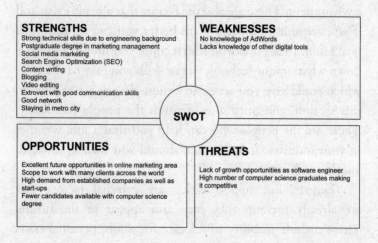

STRENGTHS
Strong technical skills due to engineering background
Postgraduate degree in marketing management
Social media marketing
Search Engine Optimization (SEO)
Content writing
Blogging
Video editing
Extrovert with good communication skills
Good network
Staying in metro city

WEAKNESSES
No knowledge of AdWords
Lacks knowledge of other digital tools

SWOT

OPPORTUNITIES
Excellent future opportunities in online marketing area
Scope to work with many clients across the world
High demand from established companies as well as start-ups
Fewer candidates available with computer science degree

THREATS
Lack of growth opportunities as software engineer
High number of computer science graduates making it competitive

In the case of Jyotishikha, there is not much risk in a career shift from software engineering to digital marketing. The SWOT would have been different if Jyotishikha did not have the postgraduate marketing qualification or if her work experience had been more than ten years.

To build a successful career, it is important to know what you are good at and the areas you need to work on. Always remember that you should not only be aware of your strengths but also your weaknesses. It is only by understanding your weaknesses that you can work to eliminate them. Similarly, if you know the threats that block your ability to move forward, you can find ways to eliminate or reduce them. Take a pen and a sheet of paper and write down your SWOT in detail, and honestly. Do not worry, no one is going to see this exercise. This is for you and for your own reference only. Please also note that this is a one-time exercise for a particular goal—your job search, in this case.

The SWOT Format

Now is the time to create your own personal SWOT based on the goal you want to achieve. You can use the following format. You can also use the many online SWOT formats that are available. Some resources for online SWOTs are available at www.swotanalysis.com. You can also use www.canva.com to prepare your own template.

Blank template to create personal SWOT

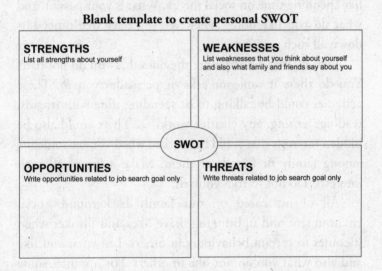

STRENGTHS
List all strengths about yourself

WEAKNESSES
List weaknesses that you think about yourself and also what family and friends say about you

SWOT

OPPORTUNITIES
Write opportunities related to job search goal only

THREATS
Write threats related to job search goal only

4. Interests, Likes and Dislikes:

Many people, after a few years in a particular career, find that this is not what they wanted to do. Boredom, lack of interest and demotivation start setting in, and a strong urge to change one's career begins to build. It is very important for everyone to do what they love and are passionate about. Only a career selection based on your interests will make you happy. If you are not happy with what you do, you will not be happy in life. So, choose a career that drives you to work every day, for reasons other than just the salary it brings.

Make a list of your high-interest and low-interest activities. High-interest activities are those you are passionate about and like doing any time. For example, in their free time, some children like to paint, some like watching TV, some enjoy playing with friends, some like to read and some like spending time on social media. What is your passion and what do you like doing whenever you have free time? List down all such activities.

Low-interest activities are the ones that you do not hate! You do these if someone asks or persuades you to. These activities could be talking to or spending time with friends, reading, writing, any creative work . . . There could also be hidden interests that could be sparked when you see someone among family or friends at them. Make a list of all such interests. Do not restrict yourself.

All of us, based on our family background, social environment and upbringing, have likes and dislikes when it comes to certain behaviours in others. List what you like and also what you do not like in others. For instance, some like the company of talkative people while others do not. Similarly, one may like assertive people and those with a sense of humour, whereas some feel offended by such people. List all your behavioural likes and dislikes, given your personality. There is no right or wrong here. This list is for you and will help you identify the kind of people you are comfortable working with. In a nutshell, it will help you choose the right career path for yourself.

Complete the following matrix:

Interests, Likes and Dislikes	
High Interest	**Low Interest**
List things that you love doing	List things that you do with interest but sometimes
Like	**Dislike**
List behavioural aspects about self and others	List behavioural aspects about self and others

Knowing yourself is an important factor in choosing your career. There are many career options available, and knowing yourself will certainly help you choose the right career in the long run.

Key Takeaways

1. Do not follow others, but choose a career in which you will be happy.
2. Do not get influenced by the career choices of others. You must choose your career based on your educational qualifications, personal attributes, SWOT and interest.

Exercise

Write down your key attributes, considering how you feel about yourself and how others perceive you. This will form the foundation of your career in the long term. List the following about yourself:

a. Educational qualifications
b. Short-term courses
c. SWOT
d. Likes and dislikes
e. High- and low-interest areas

Useful Free Tools/Sites

There are some useful tools that you can use to know yourself better. These tools will be beneficial to you as they will help you assess your personality, likes and dislikes.

1. **Career suitability tests:** We recommended the Holland Code personality types test. In this test, you will be asked to select the pictures that you prefer and reject those that you don't. You will also be asked to mention your

gender, age, country and education level. Once you have provided all this, you will get your result. The result helps you choose a career that matches your preferences, thereby increasing your chances of being successful. It also recommends some career options that offer you better chances of success. The test takes less than five minutes. You can choose the Holland Code test option at www.123test.com. It is free.

2. **TestColor:** TestColor asks you to do two things: 'Click on the colours you like most' and 'Click on the colours you like least'. TestColor provides results that tell you your emotional intelligence, your social skills, your work style, and whether you are an extrovert or introvert. This test does not take more than two minutes and can be taken at www.testcolor.com.

3. **www.crystalknows.com:** This portal provides you with one of the most popular assessment tools in the world; it does your DISC—Dominance (D), Inducement (I), Submission (S), and Compliance (C)—assessment for free. You just need to answer a few questions and you will get a report that will tell you how your personality fits into your work environment, what comes naturally to you, what energizes you, what drains you, whom you might have conflicts with, how you perceive others' behaviours and how others perceive yours.

2

How to Select the Right Job and Company (and the People Who Can Get You the Job)

'What you need to learn, children, is the difference between right and wrong in every area of life. And once you learn the difference, you must always choose the right.'

—Jeanne DuPrau

Choosing the right career for yourself is very important for your long-term success, for your sense of engagement in life, and above all, for your and your family's happiness. Due to a lack of choice or due to poor planning, many get into a job just for the sake of getting one. After a few years, they feel trapped. The reasons for their wrong choice could be many. Maybe their salaries are very high or they have niche skills with limited job opportunities, and they feel trapped wherever they are. Or maybe they are not trying enough. It is common to see people sticking to the wrong professions and regretting it for life. They have ended up in this situation because they lacked guidance and simply took up whatever job came their way. Another important reason for their distressing job situation is the lack of proper career planning on their part. Therefore, it is very important that you be conscious of your choices and plan your future career with the greatest care. After all, happiness matters more than anything else in life. Ultimately, we all work to be happy!

Now that you have done the exercises recommended in Chapter 1 (if you still have not done them, we recommend you read Chapter 1 again and complete all the self-assessment exercises before proceeding further) and are aware of your behavioural attributes, SWOT, likes, dislikes and interests, it is time to choose your job and career based on your own self-analysis. Once you know yourself, you can decide which functional areas and industries may be appropriate for you.

Never forget that the knowledge, skills and behavioural attributes required for each role and industry are different. Companies are very selective while hiring. If you choose a role and industry based on what you are and what they need, then the job search process becomes much easier.

We recommend that you make two lists: one for the functional areas where you can look for a job, and the other for the industries. You can use the format illustrated below.

Refer to your table for educational qualifications and make a list of the functional areas of your choice which are relevant to your qualifications. You must do some research to know what career options are available. Do not be generic.

Be as specific as possible. For example, marketing is too generic a choice, as marketing has many sub-functions. Some of them are:

- Marketing research
- Advertising
- Branding
- Communication
- Value-added services
- Usage and retention
- Promotion
- Social media marketing
- Product management
- Public relations

And there are many more!

The list above includes the options available only in the field of marketing. Based on your qualifications and experience, you should do your own research and make your own list. Since we all have different qualifications and work experience, this list will be different for everyone.

Once you have made the list, please refer to your SWOT, interests, likes and dislikes, and choose three or four specific roles from the list. You can use the elimination or selection method to do this. The objective is to choose three or four areas of your interest. For example, if you are an introvert and do not like social interaction, then you should not choose public relations or advertising because these roles require good interpersonal and communication skills as well as client-relations management skills. It is recommended then that you choose social media marketing, market research or product management, which are more suitable for an introvert.

Make a list of career options:	
Functional area of your choice	Role of choice in that functional area
Functional area 1	Role 1:
	Role 2:
	Role 3:
Functional area 2	Role 1:
	Role 2:
	Role 3:
Functional area 3	Role 1:
	Role 2:
	Role 3:
Make a list of minimum two functional areas and minimum two roles of choice in that functional area	

Let us take another example. For those who want to make a career in human resources, the following are some of the options to choose from:

- Talent acquisition or recruitment
- Talent management
- Learning and development
- Compensation and benefits
- Employee relations
- HR operations

- Administration
- HR generalist

These career options are available to all graduates and MBAs in human resources. But which one would be right for you? In order to answer this question, you need to understand the responsibilities, skills and attributes attached to each role.

A talent acquisition role entails identification and acquisition of skilled manpower to meet a company's current and future needs. As a talent acquisition specialist, you will be responsible for planning manpower, which will consist of identifying, sourcing, shortlisting, assessing and hiring candidates. You will also be responsible for enhancing your company's brand value and social media presence to attract the right talent and develop for your company a robust pipeline of candidates. If we get into specifics, as a talent acquisition professional, your job will include relationship building with colleges for campus recruitment, management of recruitment agencies, salary negotiations, issue of offer letters, and management of the candidates who join. In short, the talent acquisition team is responsible for all hiring activities, ranging from attracting candidates to apply to the company to overseeing their joining the company. The skill sets and behavioural attributes required to be a good talent acquisition professional include good communication and presentation skills, good MS Excel and PowerPoint skills, analytical skills, creative thinking, a collaborative attitude, relationship-building skills, negotiation skills, patience and good listening skills.

Many organizations have different roles within their talent management team. In general, these roles take care of performance management, employee productivity, employee engagement, employee retention, career progression, employee development, succession planning, employee experience and organizational culture. Within talent management, a fresher or a candidate with less than five years of work experience is given only partial responsibility, and the requirements of their job are less onerous. The talent management team is responsible for all activities related to employees, from their joining the company till their separation or retirement from it.

There is another team in HR, and that is the learning and development team. This team is responsible for building the required knowledge, skills and attitudes among employees with a view to making them highly productive in their current roles and to prepare them for various future roles within the company. The role of a learning and development professional within HR involves identification of the training and development needs of employees, planning and execution of various training interventions to build competencies, identification of internal and external partners for e-learning, coaching, mentoring and measuring effectiveness. Within this function also, a fresher starts with only a few responsibilities and initially performs only one or two roles. The attributes and interests required to be a good learning and development professional are facilitation and influencing skills, organizing skills, and presentation and communication skills.

It is noteworthy to mention here that compensation and benefits are also part of talent management in some companies. The talent management team in such companies work on salaries, employee benefits and wage data, and provide insights on salary revision and management of employee-related costs to the company. They also compare their employees' compensation and benefits with those of other companies. The idea is to ensure company employees receive the right compensation and benefits, so as to attract the best talent from the market. If you are not an extrovert and do not have good communication and presentation skills but are analytical, with good computer skills, and love to play with numbers and data, this job will be more suitable for you.

The employee relations role in HR helps prevent and resolve disputes, create and enforce policies consistently for all, and maintain a harmonious relationship between the union and the company. In some companies, this role is also responsible for maintaining all labour and statutory law compliances. This role requires good bargaining, interpersonal, influencing and networking skills, knowledge of industry and labour laws as well as a compliance orientation.

There is also an HR operations role, which involves management of payrolls, reimbursements, employee queries, all human resource information technology systems, employee files and internal and external audits, among other functions. If you are an introvert, but have good compliance orientation as well as technical, listening and conflict management skills, this role will be suitable for you.

The administration or employee services role involves maintenance and management of office vehicles and office space, factory, guest house and other official buildings.

In addition, it also involves travel management and guest entertainment. This role requires a person to be good at administrative work and to be assertive, have good liaison, public relations and negotiation skills, and be compliance oriented.

As mentioned above, there are many roles you can choose from if you want to build a career in human resources. You need to write down a list of the various roles that suit your qualifications, experience and specialization. If there is no direct match, choose the roles related to your qualifications, experience and specialization.

Once you have written down the roles suitable for you, you should refer to your personal SWOT, interests, likes and dislikes, and choose the most relevant roles from your list. If you feel that you have good analytical, reasoning and technical skills but are not an extrovert, then compensation and benefits, or HR operations, can be a better option for you than learning and development. If you like reading people, talking to them and are an extrovert, then learning and development, or recruitment, can be more suitable for you within HR. Please note that the focus should be on choosing two or three career options based on your qualifications, experience and behavioural attributes.

Identifying roles for yourself is a critical step towards ensuring that you are happy in the career you choose and do not feel pressured and demotivated after sometime. Having identified the roles for your future career, the next step is to identify your dream company and the people who can be instrumental in getting you a job in those companies.

How to Select Companies for Your Employment

Selecting the right functional area and role for yourself is very important when you search for a job. The right selection of these two critical components will also ensure that you are taking up a job that you are really passionate about. Don't forget that you are making a choice! 'Why do you want to join this company?' is a common interview question. This is an important question, and you should think about it much before the interview itself, at the time of choosing to apply for a particular job. Don't lose sight of the fact that every company wants to know why it should select you. Just as a company is interested in knowing whether you are the right fit for it, you too should think about whether the company you are seeking to join is the right fit for you.

You should select the company for your future employment based on the following three criteria:

1. Does this company hire for the role that you are looking for?
2. Is the company a long-term or short-term choice for you?
3. Is the feedback from current employees working in that company good?

1. Does this company hire for the role that you are looking for?

Do not go by big brands or top ranks when it comes to companies. The most important thing you need to know is whether or not the company hires for the role you are looking for and the skill set you possess. If the answer is yes, the company should be in your shortlist of employers. You should search on Google, LinkedIn and on one or two job sites to find out if the company is hiring for your kind of role and skill set.

2. Company history and performance

The total number of registered companies in India is 20,00,000! In 2020 alone, 36 per cent of them folded up.* Each company may offer unique advantages and its own value proposition. For the purpose of your job search, it is important that you shortlist companies that have a good history and track record of consistent performance. As you are looking for a long-term career with your company, you need to be careful when you make your choice. It should be based on the company's history, the type of business it does, its performance, its fundamentals and the founders' credentials. A strong past is an indication of a good future.

If you are a job aspirant with less than five years of work experience, we would advise you to avoid new-age start-ups that are less than two years old and are not promoted by people or institutions with a strong background. Small changes in the environment, market, funding and demand negatively

---

*   Abhishek Waghmare, 'More than 36 per cent of Registered Companies Have "Closed" Down in India', *Business Standard*, 30 July 2019, https://www.business-standard.com/article/companies/more-than-36-of-registered-companies-have-closed-down-in-india-119073000035_1.html

impact these kinds of companies, and the first action they take is against employees. Risk-taking at this juncture of your career can be fatal; hence, select companies carefully, keeping long-term job tenure in mind.

3. Company culture

Top-performing companies always believe that employees are their greatest assets. They take all steps to keep their employees engaged, productive, motivated and happy. They think long term and work on building the skills of their employees to develop their potential. These companies support the career progression of their employees, create work-life balance for them and strive to achieve an overall positive employee experience. They, in fact, promote good values, ethical practices, collaboration, open communication and transparency.

Most companies have a catchy vision, mission and values statement. You need to look beyond these statements to find out the real culture of the company. While selecting a company, you should consider factors such as employee attrition, employee engagement and the freedom of their employees to raise their voice. You can easily find out how a company fares in these areas on various social media platforms, such as Glassdoor or LinkedIn, among others. These social media sites can provide you with real and insightful information about your target company, based on which you may or may not shortlist it for your job search. For example, Glassdoor provides current and past employees' feedback on companies; you can find out what employees liked or did not like about these companies, the salaries they offer, and so on. This information, provided by people who have worked or are still working in specific companies, will help you shortlist those companies for your future employment.

Make a list of such companies. Make sure that your list has a minimum of thirty companies. The larger the list, the larger will be the market for your job search.

Identify Key People in Those Companies

After making a list of all the prospective companies for your employment, the next step is to identify people in those companies. These are the people who can help you get your desired job, now and even in the future. You should focus on making a database only of the key people who are in decision-making roles, as only they can, through their influence, help you get your job. In your list of people whom you must contact, you must also add those—apart from the decision makers—who can influence decision makers in various companies. However, please note that decision makers for you will not only be chief executive officers, managing directors or heads of HR, but also all the people involved in the recruitment process.

Example

If you have selected HR executive as one of the roles for your future employment, then for each company on your list, the list of decision makers should include the head of the department for HR, the business HR head, the plant head (if manufacturing) and the recruiter. The influencers for this role can be the HR team members of that company (two or three), officials in the labour department and key government officials of the city where the company is located. As you can see, most people are related to the function and role you have chosen. This list will be different for each role and function.

This is one of the most critical steps in the job search process and, therefore, in-depth research and preparation of the right list will ensure your success, not only in getting your next job but also in the future.

Getting a job is important, but what is more important is to get the job through ethical means. Promise yourself that you will not use unethical tactics to reach any of the key people in any company for a job. The objective is to reach the maximum number of companies and people where job vacancies may be available. Always remember that, as research has confirmed, only 15–20 per cent of vacancies get published; 80 per cent of jobs do not get advertised. With this step, your objective is to find out the maximum number of vacancies that do not get published. The more companies and right people you reach, the higher are your chances of success.

List companies of your choice for future employment	
Name of the company	Key person and influencer in the company
Company 1:	1.
	2.
	3.
	4.
	5.
	6.
Company 2:	1.
	2.
	3.
	4.
	5.
	6.
Make a list of minimum twenty companies and six or more key people or influencers for each company	

To know about the key influencers in a company, you must go through the company's website, its LinkedIn and Facebook pages, its social media feeds and news coverage in publications and run a Google search. This needs to be done for each key person in your list. Spend quality time on this research and make a note of the key points with respect to each person. Your note should include your assessment about those persons, including what they like, their interests, their views about people and other social, professional and political details about them. Make a note of all information that can give you a clue about your key persons' interests, their hobbies, likes and dislikes.

Make a list of minimum twenty companies and six or more key people or influencers for each company	
Key person and their attributes	
Name of the company:	Key attributes and information
Name of the key person 1:	1. Hobbies are yoga, painting, singing
Ramesh Birla, head, branding and communications	2. Posts quotes daily on LinkedIn
	3. Posts selfie videos (videos of his dog) frequently
	4. Posts pictures with family or self (Facebook, Instagram, Twitter)
	5. Subject on which he gives lectures or makes videos
Name of the key person 2:	1.
	2.
	3.
	4.
	5.

It is advisable to have this information about a minimum of five persons in each company. You can use the above-mentioned format to capture all relevant information.

Consider this hypothetical situation: You are studying in college and are in need of Rs 500. Whom will you ask to give you this money, or to arrange it for you? Who is more likely to give you this money? Of course, a friend or someone who knows you. There is only a remote chance that an unknown person will help you. The same is true of a job search. The idea behind knowing the right people and building a relationship with them is to approach them for help as and when there is a need. You must know that the information you have collated on key individuals will prove to be immensely useful while connecting with and influencing people to help you.

Remember, these people will be your god-sent angels in any future job search. In fact, we can assure you, the contacts you build this way will make for the most important contacts in your professional life.

The information you have collected and entered in the different tables in this chapter, as advised, will be used later in the book to further help you in your job search.

Key Takeaways

1. Know about career options available to you and choose from them after careful consideration.
2. There are many career options available that you are not even aware of. Find out what they are.
3. Most of the vacancies in companies are not publicly advertised.
4. There are influencers outside the company and key people within who can help you get your desired job.
5. Identifying influencers and building relations with them is the key to getting your dream job.

Exercise

1. Make a list of all career options available to you, based on your educational qualifications and experience, and shortlist four or five of them.
2. Make a list of thirty companies that may offer you the career options you have selected.
3. List a minimum of five key persons for each of the thirty companies (identified above), who can influence the hiring process.

Useful Free Site

My Opportunity: www.myopportunity.com helps you maximize your network. Once you upload your email contact here, they will notify you as and when people look for someone with your skill set. Though the database is more international as of now, the platform has the potential to be leveraged in India too.

3

The Ways Companies Recruit (and the Best Options for You)

'If you know the enemy and know yourself, you need not fear the result of a hundred battles. If you know yourself but not the enemy, for every victory gained, you will also suffer a defeat. If you know neither the enemy nor yourself, you will succumb in every battle.'

—*Sun Tzu*

Whether it is battle, sports or a job search that you are involved in, knowing yourself as well as your environment will help you play using your full strength while also working on your weaknesses, which will bring the desired results faster. Regardless of their experience, industry, compensation levels or country, most job seekers find the job search process extremely stressful. The whole process of customizing your application for each job, reaching out to recruiters, waiting for your interview call, worrying about your interview performance, the negotiations involved . . . all this takes time, and calls for immense patience. To make things worse, most of the time this effort does not get translated into the desired results.

Have you ever wondered why?

India may be the fastest growing market in the world, but it is a country of over 130 crore people, which also includes the largest population of youth in the world. Over 1.5 crore educated youth enter the job market every year, and the jobs available do not number even 20 per cent of this. One-third of available employment lies in the unorganized sector, and only 20 per cent of the jobs available are in the organized sector, including both the private and public sectors.[*]

---

[*] India Population 2021, Demographics, Maps, Graphs, worldpopulationreview.com; Shiv Nalapat, '"90 Million Jobs by 2030": How Pandemic Threatens to Derail Prospects of the World's Largest Youth Population', *timesnownews.com*, 27 Aug. 2020, https://www.timesnownews.com/india/article/90-million-jobs-by-2030-how-pandemic-threatens-to-derail-prospects-of-the-worlds-largest-youth-population/643508; Prakash Mallya, 'India Is Creating Millions of High Skilled Jobs, but Its Education System Isn't Keeping Up', *Forbes*, 6 May 2018, https://www.forbes.com/sites/prakashmallya/2018/05/06/india-is-creating-millions-of-high-skilled-jobs-but-its-education-system-isnt-keeping-up/?sh=3dbace2f480f

Unemployment among the educated is one of the biggest concerns for the country, and is greatly debated too. Almost 30 million graduates and 10 million postgraduates are unemployed in India. Around 47 per cent of graduates in India are not considered capable of any kind of industry role.[*] The reasons are many—their standard of education is low, they lack the right skills, their educational curricula are irrelevant and outdated, and they lack an attitude of enterprise. Additionally, there is a lack of job opportunities.

For starters, you must understand that applicants always outnumber available jobs. Companies receive, on average, 100 applications for every job they advertise. For any job posted on a job portal or social media site, an average of 1,000 job aspirants barely initiate application, 600 actually start to apply, 200 complete the application process; 100 résumés are rejected by either the application tracking system of the company or the recruiter, and only twenty résumés reach the hiring manager. In the end, only six to eight applicants will be invited for an interview, two to three for the final interview, one offered a job and one more reserved as back-up. Every job aspirant needs to know this recruitment process

[*] ET Online, '94% of Engineering Graduates Are Not Fit for Hiring, Says This IT Stalwart', *The Economic Times*, 4 June 2018, https://economictimes.indiatimes.com/jobs/only-6-of-those-passing-out-of-indias-engineering-colleges-are-fit-for-a-job/articleshow/64446292.cms; Priyamvada Grover, 'Being Highly Educated Doesn't Guarantee You Jobs in India Anymore', *ThePrint*, 26 September 2018, https://theprint.in/india/governance/being-highly-educated-doesnt-guarantee-you-jobs-in-india-anymore/125011/

and must understand that out every 1000 job aspirants, only one is offered a job!

The other and more important point to remember is that your success in this process is not entirely dependent upon you. You must also understand the way recruitment is done. You need to know the other side of the story—the inside story of how recruitment is done. Once you know it, the whole process of looking for a job will become easier, faster and more enjoyable.

Know How Companies Recruit

Each company has its own strategy to reach the right candidates and follows its own hiring process. The idea is to recruit candidates with the relevant knowledge, skills and attitude, who can fit in with their culture. The first step on the part of any company is to advertise its vacancies and invite applications for them.

Companies use the following ways to recruit people:

1. Newspaper advertisements
2. Job fairs
3. Walk-in interviews
4. Direct or forced applications
5. Job portals
6. Company website
7. Hackathons (mostly for technical jobs)
8. References
9. Internal/employee referrals
10. Professional networking sites

Not all these means of recruitment may be useful to you. Research by www.cxomentors.com shows that companies do 29 per cent of their hires through employee reference, 26 per cent through social media and job sites, 11 per cent on campuses, only 3 per cent through advertisements in print media; and 32 per cent of their hiring is done through other channels. Hence, focusing on and applying through all hiring channels is a waste of time and energy. You should, instead, focus on a few hiring channels that will give you the desired results, with less effort on your part and in a short period of time.

Newspaper job advertisements are preferred by governments, public sector undertakings, and local companies; larger enterprises too employ this method for mass recruitment or for hiring for any specific areas. Most newspapers carry small advertisements in their classifieds section and also dedicate a full page to careers on a particular day of the week. Some newspapers also have dedicated job supplements where they carry a large number of vacancy advertisements from various companies. Advertising in the classifieds section of a newspaper is cost effective, as newspapers charge per word. A small advertisement of thirty to fifty words costs very little and is preferred by local and small companies for hiring. This means of advertising is useful for those looking for jobs in smaller towns, cities and regions, as most of the regional newspapers carry advertisements for jobs in their local areas of readership. For example, there are the newspapers *Anandabazar Patrika* and *Telegraph* for Kolkata, *New Indian Express, Samaja* and *Dharitri* for Bhubaneswar and Cuttack, *Dainik Jagran, Aaj* and *Hindustan* for Patna, *Vijay Karnataka* for Bengaluru, and

Amar Ujala and *Dainik Jagran* for Kanpur. If your preference is for a local, average salary job, then job advertisements in the regional newspapers may be a good source of leads for you. Mid-sized and large companies publish job advertisements in the newspapers more for branding purposes than with the objective of hiring, as newspaper advertisements encourage a large number of people to apply and it is very difficult for any company to go through so many applications for shortlisting. Most of the large companies that advertise in newspapers are those from the IT, ITES, e-commerce, bank, insurance and retail industries, which hire in large numbers. Through the newspaper advertisement, they get a large number of applicants; they are directed to submit their profiles to the company's career portal, where an automated system filters the relevant applications that meet the company criteria. In the current age of social media, all newspaper advertisements for jobs are also available on companies' online portals. In this day and age, scanning many newspapers for the vacancy you desire is time-consuming and a less effective way to search for a job.

Job fairs—also called career fairs or career expos—are events where a large number of companies participate. Generally, they are looking to attract a large number of job aspirants to interact with face-to-face and get them to submit their résumés for potential recruitment. A job fair is usually organized in a college auditorium or ground, or in a city exhibition space. In the current digital times, online or virtual job fairs are also quite frequent. An online or virtual career fair includes many features such as video and live chats, making it easier for both job recruiter and seeker. Job fairs are popular among colleges, and are suited for mass hiring of freshers. For companies, it is a cost-effective way to reach out to a large number of job seekers or applicants. It is time-effective as well as an indirect way to market their own company brand. The job fair is quite popular for mass hiring at entry level by the hospitality, real estate, insurance, BPO, security, direct sales, retail and e-commerce companies.

But when the number of applicants is very large, the job fair can result in competition and stress. More often than not, job fairs are used for company branding and as a brand promotion exercise rather than for actual hiring. The job fair may be of some help to fresh graduates seeking entry-level jobs and to those passing out from higher secondary school. But for a professionally qualified job aspirant, the job fair is not an effective means of searching for a job.

Walk-in interviews are organized by a company at its own premises or sometimes at another place to fill mass vacancies in quick time. Like the job fair, walk-ins are organized for freshers or for less experienced candidates, to enable quick, cost-effective recruiting in large numbers. The advantage for the applicant is that the results are known on the same day, and the interview can be attended on the weekend. You may have to bargain for a lower salary from such recruitment, as the number of applicants is usually large. For the same reason, you may also waste a lot of time waiting for your turn, and may end up feeling frustrated and demotivated.

Direct or forced job application is when a job aspirant sends his or her résumé for consideration when there is no vacancy advertised. A forced application can be done by sending in a hard copy of one's résumé or by email or through social media portals like LinkedIn. Many of you must be sending out forced applications on LinkedIn or by email to your connections, asking for help. We have seen that most such aspirants just attach their résumés and request that they be considered for a suitable job. Remember, like you, there will be many who must be sending in applications like this. First, if the connection does not know you, the chances of your even getting a response are very slim. Or, you might get a standard response, such as, 'I will revert to you', 'Sure', 'I will let you know', and you will never hear back from them. Second, even if the person at the other end genuinely wants to help you, he will not have time or will not make the effort to open your résumé and read the details to see how he can help. So, if you want to send a forced application, then you must send a customized one in simple language with clearly written contact details. Do mention in brief your qualifications, experience and what help you expect from the recipient of your request. Be brief and crisp. Most will not open your attachment and take the time and effort to help you. If you want to use the forced application at all, then you should make a list of target recipients, as explained earlier, and write to them. Be persistent and follow up with them if you want them to help. Some may revert if they see regular follow-ups from you. The forced application method has limitations, and requires consistent effort with targeted and familiar people to get you any success.

Applying on job or company portals is the most popular means of job search among aspirants today. It is convenient for companies as it attracts a large number of applicants; companies also have new technologies that help shortlist the relevant profiles. As a job applicant, you can, from the comfort of your home, access thousands of jobs and apply for them any time from anywhere. You can search for job openings compatible with your qualifications, experience, interests and the companies of your choice anywhere in the world, with a click of the mouse. It is economical, less time-consuming than other means of applying for a job, and convenient for all the stakeholders. These exact features are its disadvantages too! Because, like you, there are thousands using the same route and applying for the very job you are applying for. This just increases the competition. Since anyone can apply through the job portal, this mode attracts a lot of ineligible applicants too, and your chances of getting the job depend on the probability of your profile being noticed. Sometimes, these job seekers are prime targets for scammers. They pose as prospective employers and ask for their personal information, such as phone numbers, addresses, PAN and Aadhaar number, using which they can proceed to cheat them of money. We have reported many frauds where job aspirants like you have paid thousands of rupees to scamsters for interviews, as 'registration fee', 'processing fee', etc. We advise you that anyone who is asking for money in the name of recruitment is a fraud. No company charges money from aspirants for recruitment. We also find that most job aspirants lose precious long hours browsing for relevant jobs and applying without much success.

A **hackathon** (derived from words 'hack' and 'marathon') is a collaborative software and hardware development event organized by companies to hire technical manpower by testing for practical and real technical skills. The American tech companies started using hackathons to generate new ideas or to develop prototypes or products from their existing ideas within a short period of one or two days. Companies promote their hackathons on social media, and this helps them in their branding and in promoting themselves as innovative. This concept is picking up and becoming popular in India for the hiring of technical and niche skills for companies. If you are looking for a technical job, you should explore hackathons for experience and exposure. This method of hiring is used by a few companies and for limited niche skills. It may not be useful for most of you.

Choosing the Best Method for Yourself

Use the 80:20 rule. You need to focus on methods that will get you the desired long-term results with less effort. On average, the tenure range of most employees at a company is four to five years. Hence, you need to spend your time, effort and energy on methods and tools that can give you repeated results.

Most job aspirants do not have a strategy. They apply for all job vacancies that come their way in one or more ways mentioned above. This approach may bring results to some. But for most, this results in frustration, demotivation and the shattering of their confidence.

Just as each company has its own recruitment strategy to hire the best candidates, each job aspirant too should have a job search plan unique and specific to his or her needs. What should such a plan consist of? This is discussed in detail in the next chapter.

We recommend that you completely ignore the first seven methods, as the probability of your getting results from them, in comparison to the effort they call for, will be very low. Also, you will find that there is too much competition if you take these routes.

In the year 1996, after passing out with an engineering degree, Subir was looking for a job. He used to look for vacancy advertisements in the newspapers. He would buy the *Economic Times* and *The Hindu* on Tuesdays, the *Times of India* on Wednesdays, and the local newspapers on other days of the week. He used to clip out the relevant vacancy advertisements and apply against each. In the following six months, Subir applied for more than 500 jobs! Do you know what the results were? Forget a job, he did not even get an acknowledgement from any company.

Now that we are in this domain and reasonably experienced, we realize that companies advertise in the newspapers more for branding and for building a database than to fill any vacancies they may have. We can understand that it is difficult for companies too to handle applications fetched by this method. Unemployment in the country is high, and for each vacancy advertised, companies receive applications in the thousands. It is practically very difficult to acknowledge and send responses to all. One lesson learnt then, in the nineties, and which is true for today's job aspirants too, is that newspaper advertisements are not worth the hard work they entail for the purpose of searching for a job. Responding to job advertisements in the newspapers works only if you are looking for government or public sector jobs. For example, all central government jobs are advertised on https://www.upsc.gov.in/, and there are similar sites for public sector undertaking (PSU) recruitment and for state government jobs.

You will find one thing in common across the first seven of the ten recruitment mediums listed earlier; the seven are: newspaper advertisements, job fairs, direct applications, job portals, walk-in interviews, company websites and hackathons. The common feature is that they invite mass applications. We strongly recommend that you avoid these seven mediums. Each has its own merits and demerits, of course. However, we want you to focus on the mediums that give better results, and with less effort on your part.

Now that we have eliminated seven of the ten modes of job search, let us focus on the three that will give you results in minimum time and with comparatively less effort.

It is important to understand how these three mediums work. Once you understand the tricks of the game, it will be easier for you to focus on those areas to maximize results.

How to Use 'External References'

Reference is the most effective way to land a job! It is easy, quick and effective, and carries the highest chances of success. You need to know and be able to get key external or internal people to recommend your case to the right person in your target company. We would give high priority to this medium of job search, and you must learn to use it if you wish to have faster success.

External references are key people outside the organization who are influential and can influence the hiring decision makers in the company where you want a job. They can be both people in high and influential positions as well as people who know influential people in the company whose support could be life-changing for you.

How to Identify Key External References, and Ways to Seek Their Support

Let us understand this with a real-life example:

Rohan is an electrical engineer with no work experience. He has just passed out from college. In India, 15 lakh students pass out from engineering colleges every year, and only 20 per cent of them get a job that is compatible with their qualifications. Like the remaining 80 per cent who do not, Rohan too did not get a campus placement. He is looking for a job in the core electrical engineering field. Rohan, who lives in Nagpur, also has location constraints and cannot relocate to another city for a job.

Let us find out how Rohan can identify external references for his job search.

Rohan needs to identify his target companies and make a list of all the companies in his city and in nearby places where he prefers to work. The table below illustrates how Rohan can identify the right companies for himself or just make a list of companies likely to suit his aspirations. He should then make a list of influential people in the city whom he knows or can approach through family and friends. He can also use the help of local politicians and the extended network of his friends to expand the list further. This list should be as exhaustive as it can be so that, after the process of elimination, you still have some people who could really be helpful to you.

Once his list is ready, Rohan needs to evaluate it and select people who fulfil all the criteria below:

1. They must be currently in position of influence or power.
2. The companies selected by Rohan should be within the area of their influence.
3. These people's cooperation is needed by the companies for more efficient operation.

This list will be different for each job aspirant, of course, based on the job being looked for.

Let us take the example of an MBA in human resources looking for a job in HR. The list of people for reference could be the human resource adviser in a local area or some local firm that is working with the company. The idea is to find vacancies that do not get advertised and people who have more information about the company will help you find those vacancies. In this way, you will be exposed to more vacancies, thus increasing your chances.

We are not advising you to use any unethical means or get these people to pressure companies to give you a job. But you will use them or their reference to take your profile to the concerned person in your target companies for consideration, which would be a daunting task in itself otherwise. Making the right list of influencers is important, and you can use the table below to make your reference list.

Table for your reference list:

References							
		Contact details			Whom he can influence		
Name of the person	Position	Phone no.	Email ID	Company name	Person in the company	Position in the company	Note of reference

You might ask, but why would they help you when they do not even know you?

Well, they have helped others and will help you too. You need to work on building and nurturing your relationship with each of your influencers. How you can do this has been covered in detail in the subsequent chapters.

How to Use Internal/Employee Referrals for Job Search

Employees currently working in companies where you are looking for a job would know about current and future vacancies even before they are advertised to the outside world. Most companies have an internal job posting (IJP) and employee referral programme for sourcing résumés and filling vacancies. Jobs are advertised outside only if a company is not able to fill its vacancies through its internal sources and employee referrals.

Current employees in any company would also know who the hiring manager and the heads responsible for hiring are. These internal employees of a company are your most critical sources of reference in finding a job. A right approach, connection with and support from these internal people in a company will ensure that you not only get the job but also have someone to hand-hold you while settling in the company and ensure your success after your recruitment too.

Companies too prefer to hire through employee referrals as it is considered one of the most productive recruiting strategies. Research has proven that referred employees are the best employees in many ways. Companies prefer employee referral hiring for the following reasons:

a.   **Better quality of hire:** Referrals are an internal method of finding candidates. Here, existing employees are asked to refer candidates for the open positions in the company. Existing employees, having knowledge of the roles, the company and the cultural fitment requirements, are likely to recommend the appropriate candidates. This is why candidates hired through employee referrals are a much better match for company requirements than candidates coming from other sources.

b.   **High retention and high engagement:** Because they make a better match from the outset, referred employees often stay longest with the company. Employees who match the organizational norms, culture and values better, naturally stay longer with the company. Not only the new hires, but employees who successfully referred them have also been found to stay longer with their companies than those who have not referred any candidates. Employees who refer candidates also have a sense of achievement and feel they have done something useful for the company they work for. Both the referrer and the referred have a sense of belonging, and statistics have shown that both are much more engaged and productive compared with other employees. High retention and high engagement are a dream human resource matrix and impact all parameters of an organization and benefit all stakeholders.

c. **Reduced time and cost of recruitment**: Often, referred employees, who learn about a company from current employees, are familiar with the hiring and onboarding process. Not only does the company get their profiles and contact information quickly, but it also hires and takes them on board much faster. Since the time to hire is shorter, the cost to hire also drops. The company needs fewer human hours to fill a position, and this automatically makes hiring more productive and efficient. In addition, when the company knows that referrals make the best employees, they reduce their dependency on other, costly sources of hiring, like job portals and advertisements.

d. **Improved employer brand**: Research by LinkedIn, www.cxomentors.com and many other job surveys have shown that 75 per cent of job seekers read about the company's brand and reputation before they apply for an open position there.* Employee referrals are an endorsement of the employer brand.

How to Identify Key Internal References and Seek Their Attention

Roshni has just acquired an MBA in marketing and has no work experience. More than 3 lakh students pass out every

---

* ultimate-list-of-employer-brand-stats.pdf, LinkedIn.com

year from more than 5000 management colleges in India. Like the engineering students, only 20 per cent find appropriate placements; 80 per cent either do not get a job at all, or take up jobs that require only a non-engineering graduate degree. Roshni is one among them.

Let us see how Roshni can use the internal reference channel to find a job.

Marketing is too broad a career option for any fresher to consider as a whole. Roshni needs to first decide on two or three career options or roles within marketing so that her search for internal references is focused. You can refer to Chapter 1: 'How to Choose a Career', for more details on how to make a plan for yourself.

Say, Roshni has decided to make a career in business development. Let us also assume that she has limitations and cannot move to the metros like Delhi or Mumbai. She, therefore, has selected only two cities, Patna, her home city, and Kolkata, for her job search. Since her choice of career and location are decided, she should now make a list of all her target companies. She may use the tools and techniques mentioned in the relevant sections above to identify companies for herself. Now, she should prepare the list of people who will have decisive influence in recruitment in those companies in her list. Roshni will have to use social media (LinkedIn, Facebook, Twitter, Google, company pages and company social media pages) and research those companies extensively to make her list of internal influencers. She should keep the following things in mind while making this list:

1. The people on her list should be at a high level of hierarchy in those companies.
2. They should be working in the function in which Roshni is looking for a role.
3. If the company has a presence at many locations, then the list should comprise senior leaders at the company's regional offices (relevant to Roshni) and head office.

Roshni, for example, has selected a leading banking company with its head office in Mumbai, and her choice of job locations are Patna and Kolkata. She should include, in her list of influential persons, the managing director, the chief executive officer, the senior management team and the functional head of the department at the corporate level for her targeted role. At the same time, she should identify senior leaders and key people working in the sales and HR functions at Kolkata and Patna. These leaders could be the business/regional/zonal heads or the HR managers/heads in Patna and Kolkata.

This list will, of course, be different for each job aspirant, depending on their own profile and the profile of the jobs they are looking for. Focused research for selection of the right people is critical; hence, you must spend some time on this.

Follow Your Boss

For those aspirants who are already in a job, one of the easiest ways to find another job could be to follow your boss. Joining a new company by following your boss there has its own positives and negatives. Some may term this as nepotism, favouritism, or talent poaching from the first company. You may even end up burning bridges with your current company. But we have seen many success stories among employees who have followed their boss, right from entry to leadership levels. After all, you always need a mentor to find a job and grow in it.

There are advantages and disadvantages in following your boss. If you are taking up a new job, it is a fresh beginning and your past laurels do not mean anything. Moving with your boss eliminates the need to prove yourself to your new boss. You will continue to enjoy the patronage of your earlier boss. Settling down in the new company will be much easier than if you take up a job independently. A move with your boss may also come with a promotion or an increase in salary for you. You will be one of the first to be considered when it comes to job assignments or internal opportunities since your boss knows you better than your other team members whom you are new to. Also, your boss has a much better perspective of the market and knows the upside of the new environment better, thus decreasing your overall risk at the new company. The biggest advantage is that you will get peace of mind, as you already know the management style and will not have to work hard to know and adapt to a new boss's style and meet her expectations. Some bosses are nurturing by temperament and take care of their team members' career aspirations along with their own.

Moving with your boss also has some disadvantages, especially if you like your current job and are a good performer. The move may leave you branded (as your boss's attachment), and may mean your forgoing other relationships that you have developed in your present role. Another risk is that your boss's attitude towards you and his management style may change in the new company. Your boss was both supportive and flexible in the current company because circumstances at your current company may have allowed that kind of approach. But if your boss's new job is a lot more stressful and comes with far more demands, his style might change, and most of the stress may quickly filter down to you too. The new team in your new company will consider you as the boss's man, will be up against you from day one, and you will have to work extra hard to get support and reduce heartburn in office. Some bosses are also very self-centred and think of their own benefits all the time; they prefer to move with their team to get all the support they can but do not take care of the team.

Moving with your boss may be a good step to getting a better role and better compensation, if you really trust your boss. You should not, however, move under pressure or out of desperation. Even though we have seen that moving with the boss has more advantages than disadvantages, it should be a well-thought-out decision, keeping in mind all aspects. It should certainly not come across as a desperate move.

If you think from a long-term career perspective, you should consider moving with your boss only under these conditions:

- There is excellent rapport between the two of you
- Your boss allowed you freedom and supported you in challenging times
- You both connect well outside of work too
- Your boss helped you in fulfilling your career aspirations

Key Takeaways

1. Know the hiring channels through which a company recruits people.
2. Focus on three of the ten channels of hiring to maximize your results.
3. Identify external references who can help you in finding your job.
4. Identify the internal people at the company where you are looking for a job.
5. Keep in mind the points mentioned in the chapter while shortlisting your external and internal references list.
6. Keep in mind the conditions under which it will be advantageous to move to another company with your boss.

Exercise

1. Break down your career options and decide on two or three roles for focused job search.
2. Make a list of external references who can help you find a job in your target company.
3. Make a list of internal references in the company where you are looking for a job.
4. Make a list of fifty internal and external references, each related to the company you are interested in.

Useful Free Sites/Groups

1. **www.almaconnect.com**: People with some common connect will always be the first to help you. AlmaConnect

is a private alumni network focused on helping a job aspirant get trusted help from his/her alumni network. Joining this group and connecting with known circles will be useful.

2. **www.referhire.com**: Through this portal, you can connect with peers in your target companies and discover hidden jobs posted by them. You can also get clarifications on any questions you may have about these jobs. You can actually get these peers to help you with the application process.

3. **LinkedIn groups**: Join a LinkedIn group which has your identified people and companies on your list. Connect with and contribute in the group to catch their attention so that you can later ask them to refer you for a job.

4. **Facebook groups**: Join a Facebook group where your identified companies are members. You will receive information related to the companies and their job updates. You should also be active with your likes and comments so as to be noticed in the group.

4

How to Best Use Job Portals and Job Aggregators

Once you have completed researching your chosen industry and companies, it is time for you to create a strategy for connecting with those companies and bringing yourself to their notice. Creating a social strategy helps you target the right people in the most appropriate way. This increases the visibility of your professional profile, and also your chances of being spotted by recruiters who are scanning social media to find the right candidates. It not only saves you time, but also gets you maximum results with minimum effort. In short, a solid social media strategy for your job search allows you to establish your social brand, network with people online and identify leads that can be converted into job opportunities.

Social Media and Its Advantages in Searching for a Job

92 per cent of companies use social media for hiring, and three out of four hiring managers check out a candidate's social

media profile before making a hiring decision.* Competing in the modern, ultra-competitive job market now requires that you learn and master the ins and outs of social media. While traditional sites such as naukri.com, monster.com and jobsahead.com continue their reign in the job marketplace, you need to supplement these with a more diverse set of social networking sites. Strategic use of both social media and job search sites can expand your ability to uncover opportunities in ways unheard of just a few years ago. Using social media to find a job is easier than you think.

Job Portals and Job Aggregators

A high penetration of smartphones and computers and easy data availability at cheaper tariffs have digitally empowered people in India. In today's digitally charged world, it won't be an exaggeration to say that the world is in our hands. Digital technology has also touched the job industry, and a large number of job portals now advertise vacancies available in various companies. In fact, job portals have millions of jobs posted on them every month. A job portal allows employers and job seekers to post online advertisements and résumés easily. It offers search filters, such as location, qualification, experience, company and salary, which make

---

* Kimberlee Morrison, 'Survey: 92% of Recruiters Use Social Media to Find High-Quality Candidates', *Adweek*, 22 September 2015, https://www.adweek.com/performance-marketing/survey-96-of-recruiters-use-social-media-to-find-high-quality-candidates/

it easier for job seekers to find jobs relevant to them. A job seeker can create and upload online CVs and cover letters at once, which can then be easily used to apply for an unlimited number of vacancies. It appears that job portals are among the best and most efficient means by which to search for opportunities sitting at home. It won't be wrong to say that digital transformation has brought jobs and job applicants together on a common platform now.

Just as job portals are useful to job seekers, they provide significant benefits to companies too. They help companies reduce their employee search costs and hiring time. A company can now post as many vacancies as it wants, every day. It can also easily source and shortlist a large number of profiles, which used to take days earlier.

There is, however, a downside too. Since most portals offer services free to job aspirants, they are overcrowded with millions of profiles. As a matter of fact, companies receive thousands of profiles for each vacancy they post. This has dramatically reduced the overall effectiveness of job search portals.

If you want to use job portals at all in your job search, we would recommend that you devote not more than 20 per cent of your job search time to them. Use the following strategies for effective use of job search portals:

- **Use a maximum of two job search sites:** There are more than 100 job search portals in India alone. Most of them will carry similar job posts. Applying on each job portal will be a waste of your precious time; hence, select no more than two job sites from among the most popular ones, like Naukri, Monster, Indeed, JobsAhead, TimesJobs, Freshersworld, Shine, Placement India, etc. We would also caution you to not expect immediate results from applying on these sites, as a very large number of applications are received for each job posted on these platforms. You need to be mentally prepared, as it can be quite unsettling, frustrating and demotivating, to have most of your applications go unanswered.

- **Keep your résumé simple, attractive and different:** Your résumé represents you and it is the only document that can get you an interview call. The key is to write what the company is looking for. Keep it simple, error-free, attractive and different so that it catches the attention of the recruiter. Be entrepreneurial and unique, and do not copy the format from your friends or from the Internet.

- **Treat your social media profile as a CV and keep it updated:** You must complete your profile on your social media sites so that any recruiter visiting your profile gets to know about your education, experience, skills and achievements. If you are working and want to hide your intention to get a new job from your current employer, then use the hide/show or other similar feature. This feature enables you to hide your profile and status from your current employer or from selected companies.

- **Do not show desperation:** Avoid writing 'immediately available to join' or 'serving notice period'. Every recruiter wants people who are happy and not desperately looking for jobs. Most assume that there is something wrong with you if you are too desperate. Remember, this perception may get your profile rejected at the screening stage itself.

- **Update your profile and cover letter:** Update your résumé regularly, at least every three months. You must also create a cover letter highlighting your key achievements, which will immediately catch the attention of any employer. Your résumé and cover letter must have your contact details and should be error-free. We recommend Google Docs (which is free) for drafting your résumé, which can then be saved on Google Drive and exported as a PDF document when you need to apply for jobs online. It is recommended that you save your résumé as 'Résumé', followed by your full name, and the current date for making it easier for you as well as recruiters to identify.

- **Use keywords in your résumé:** There are millions of résumés on job sites, and it is important for your résumé to feature among the top search results when recruiters begin their selection. A recruiter uses key search filters to find profiles relevant to his or her requirements. Keywords are words that describe the job you want to apply for. For example, if the job description states that the recruiter needs excellent influencing collaboration and presentation skills, please incorporate these words in your profile. It will help your résumé show up to the recruiter for further review. The use of relevant keywords will ensure that your résumé features in search results. Use some of the same words and phrases in your résumé that appear in the job requirements posted by the company. The computer algorithm will then recognize your résumé as a good match and move your résumé up in the search results. Some companies also use an application tracking system to filter and shortlist relevant profiles from the database. They too use keywords. If your résumé has keywords, then it will show up in the search results of that recruitment software as well. A résumé without keywords will not show up in search results. Hence, it is very important that your résumé contains the relevant keywords.

- **Use filters and keywords to search:** The large number of jobs on the myriad job portals in existence may leave you confused and overwhelmed. You will not know which one to apply for. Finding job vacancies relevant to you is the key to saving time. Use search filters as such location, experience, company, salary, designation and skills to find the most relevant job for yourself. Apply where you meet the required criteria. Randomly applying for jobs will not only waste your time but also add to your frustration due to the poor response you will fetch from recruiters.

- **Use Advanced Search features:** Reviewing job postings and applying for jobs can be very time-consuming. Using advanced search features on job search sites can help you save time and get better results. Advanced search will let you enter multiple criteria rather than just a job title, a few keywords or a location. For example, advanced job search capabilities will allow you to limit keywords in several ways and specifically search vacancies based on company name, job type, salary, location, and how long the job has been posted.

- **Create job alerts:** Once you have identified the job search engines that are most beneficial for you, create job alerts based on the kind of job you are looking for. For example, you can create a job alert for marketing manager with two to four years' work experience in Mumbai. You can create a job alert on any site quickly and easily, based on your requirements, and can also decide on the frequency (daily, weekly, monthly) of job notifications entering your mailbox. Setting up alerts means that you will receive notifications via email or text when job openings that meet your specified criteria are posted on the sites.

- **Use a combination of methods for better results:** Recruiters are generally avalanched by résumés, and therefore your résumé will not get any extra attention as the recruiters do not know you. This may result in your résumé being rejected. It is advised that once you have applied for a job on a portal, send a personalized email (in most cases the job posted will come with an email ID) to the recruiter with your résumé attached. This will catch his or her attention and increase your chances of being called for an interview. If the email ID is not mentioned in the job posting, then do some research on the company on Google or LinkedIn and send a personalized email after finding the recruiter's or an HR team member's details.

- **Be selective to find a relevant job:** You should apply only for those roles and to those companies that you are really interested in and are in line with your career goal. It is very easy to get carried away and fill scores of applications. This will waste your time and also add to your frustration.

- **Use job portals to find jobs, and use companies' career pages to apply:** Many companies' application tracking system (ATS) may not be integrated with the job portals. Applications received through portals will not be in the priority lot due to their large numbers. The career section on the company's website is integrated with the ATS and has the capability to shortlist a few relevant profiles based on keywords, to make the task of recruiters easier. Hence, this is the preferred way to shortlist résumés, rather than shortlisting from any job portal. We recommend that you view vacancies on job portals and then go to the career page on the corresponding company's website and submit your application.

- **Use information on job portals to build your network for your benefit:** Most vacancies on the job portals have recruiters' email IDs. You should use this to your advantage, to build a long-term network and also to approach them for current unadvertised vacancies. Use social networking sites like LinkedIn, Facebook and Twitter to find recruiters and use their email IDs to connect with them. This approach helps you to reach the right person directly so that you can seek his or her support for current as well as future requirements in the company.

Most companies or search consultants, instead of using the database of the applications received, use job portals to search for candidates based on their requirements. The database of the applications received is not used as the primary source for the shortlisting of candidates, as more than 80 per cent of the profiles received are either spam or non-relevant. With an increase in job applicants on job portals, which are also increasing in number, the portals' effectiveness is also in question. We feel that there are better and more effective ways for job aspirants to search for employment; hence, we recommend that you spend limited time on job portals. Rather than job portals, networking sites are highly effective, and therefore, recommended.

Use Job Search Aggregators Rather than Job Sites

When you are in the market for a new job, using job search engines to look for openings is a good strategy. With so many sites out there, though, it's important to focus your efforts on a few that are most likely to feature the kinds of jobs that you are interested in. Otherwise, you could spend all of your time combing through site after site rather than actively applying for jobs and preparing for interviews.

We recommend the use of job aggregators instead of job portals. Job portals are like your neighbourhood marketplace where you visit ten different shops to buy groceries for the home, whereas job aggregators are like a supermarket, where everything is available under one roof.

Job sites are websites where employers post jobs directly on the portal. Naukri, Jobsahead, Monster, etc., are in this category. Job aggregators, on the other hand, are search engines that compile job postings from a wide range of websites, including job boards, into a single, searchable online interface. They aggregate all jobs from other sites and include paid job advertisements too. This option provides you with all jobs at one place, and you will not need to waste your time on individual portals. Indeed.com and LinkedIn Jobs can be good options to start with. You may even find that one (or a few) of these sites are sufficient for your needs. That's because these sites work behind the scenes to identify jobs posted elsewhere online (such as companies' career pages and other places where employers advertise jobs); additionally, they accept paid job advertisements.

Advantages of Using Job Aggregators Vs Job Portals

- **They are more comprehensive and offer greater convenience:** The function of a job aggregator is to find relevant positions from every place on the Internet and put them all in one place for the convenience of its users. It offers job seekers a more comprehensive collection of jobs. Job aggregators are gaining popularity because of the convenience they offer to job aspirants. They provide a single interface that offers the widest and comprehensive job search experience, doing away with the need for the aspirant to visit many different job sites.
- **They save your time by doing away with duplication:** Aggregators are like e-commerce shopping portals, where everything is available and you can buy as per your need instead of visiting different sites for apparel, electronics, food, etc. They consolidate job postings into a single site, streamlining your search into a single website.
- **They contain hidden jobs too:** Because aggregators search beyond job boards, they provide an opportunity to aspirants to find available positions that they would not

otherwise have found from a more standard job board search. One of these hidden positions could be your dream job!

Working Job Aggregators to Your Advantage

- **Use keywords for your job search**: Choosing a proper job keyword is essential. Recruiters use keywords in their job postings to reach the maximum number of job aspirants. You can use Google's Keyword Planner to ascertain the keyword that will find the most relevant jobs for you.
- **Maximize keyword density in your search**: Once you have selected the proper keyword, you need to make sure you use it throughout in your job search. The higher the keyword density in your search, the higher the probability of your getting relevant vacancies at the top of job aggregator searches. Make sure your keyword is included in the job title.
- **Choose the right location for your desired position**: Job aggregators enable candidates to search for positions by location. Therefore, you should always search the relevant locations for jobs. For example, if your job search location is outside of a major city's limits, then you should also use the nearest bigger city in your search. By utilizing the nearest metro city as your job's location, you can be sure that all jobs in your city too will appear in the search results.

Social media is a big time-waster; hence, you must narrow your search to find the results you need. We recommend that you use one job site, either Naukri or Monster; one job aggregator, Indeed; and one social networking site, LinkedIn.

Key Takeaways

1. Focus more on job search aggregators than on job sites.
2. Edit and use the 'Settings' feature if you are actively searching for a job.
3. Treat your profile as your CV and keep it updated.
4. Use advanced search features.
5. Create job alerts.

Exercise

1. Complete your social media profiles, specially on LinkedIn and Facebook.
2. Create a job alert for role, location and other criteria on job aggregators LinkedIn and Facebook.
3. Use the advanced search feature to familiarize yourself with it.
4. Browse Google's Keyword Planner to understand keywords for your job search.

Useful Free Sites

1. **LinkedIn Jobs**: This is the largest professional networking site globally. It aggregates job listings from thousands of websites, including job boards, staffing firms, associations and companies' career pages. You must create a job search alert on this to receive daily or weekly job vacancies.

2. **www.indeed.com:** Indeed is one of the world's largest job aggregators. You can use this to search for jobs and also to create your profile to apply faster against vacancies. It also has a section consisting of job vacancies from the best employers to help you choose better employers.

3. **www.careerjet.co.in:** This portal provides you with job information based on criteria such as sector, location, type, including private sector, government and other jobs, at one place.

4. **LinkUp:** If you are looking for jobs in the United States, then this is a useful aggregator. This pulls jobs exclusively from company websites. Therefore, all of the jobs included in a LinkUp search are reliable. For this reason, many prefer LinkUp to other aggregators.

5

Professional Networking Sites or Job Portals

Candidate profiles on job portals are not public, which makes it easier for candidates to post wrong information and make false claims about their qualifications, skills and work experience. This has reduced the credibility and effectiveness of job portals, both for companies as well as the candidates. Against this, professional networking sites are public, and profiles on them can be seen by all, including people in your current company. This minimizes the chances of applicants making fake claims. Information about a candidate's skills, videos, photos, projects, recommendations and endorsements by others on professional networking portals provide an all-round perspective of a prospective candidate to any employer. The credibility of professional networking sites has encouraged most employers to trust these sites for their search for candidates and for posting vacancies.

We recommend the use of professional networking sites in two ways: First, to find job vacancies, and second, to connect and build relationships with people who will help you find jobs.

In this segment, we shall be focusing more on how to use professional networking sites to find job vacancies. The use of these sites to build relationships and make mentors for life is described in a subsequent chapter.

Some of the Benefits of Using Professional Networking Sites in Your Job Search

- You can market yourself without being seen as a job aspirant.
- You can create positive public relations by presenting testimonials, endorsements and presentations of your work on your social media accounts, blog and/or website.
- You can build your network and engage with a wider audience across multiple social channels.
- You can apply for advertised roles easily and quickly.
- You are more visible to recruiters who are using social media to advertise their jobs and source candidates.
- You can speak to recruiters, headhunters and prospective employers throughout your job search by engaging with them across all channels in real time.

Companies Hire More Using Professional Networking Portals than Job Sites

Every company wants to hire the best talent. It is a common perception that good talent does not consist of active job seekers. Job portals mainly have the profiles of active job seekers. Those who are not looking for a job (the passive job seekers) are hard to find on job portals, whereas on professional networking sites, candidates can update their profiles without being looked upon as job seekers. This makes most companies and job seekers depend more on social networking portals than pure job sites.

Usually, job portals have poor database quality. Old and un-updated profiles of job seekers frustrate companies as they need to verify each profile after sourcing it. On the other hand, profiles on social networking sites are immediately updated upon any job change, skill enhancement, certification or achievement.

Companies leverage the advantages of 'share', 'like', 'comment' and other features to reach out to candidates in compounding numbers, which is not possible with job portals. This also helps companies attract new profiles through referrals, which is the best source of hiring.

Social networking sites have a format and pattern in which one needs to submit one's profile. This pattern is uniform for everyone, which makes it easier for companies to easily search for relevant profiles. On the other hand, the profiles in the databases of job portals are in various formats, and this makes the task of a recruiter very tough.

Job networking sites also provide qualitative feedback about every person listed on them. Endorsements, recommendations, comments, likes and posts give valuable and quality insights into any profile, which is missing in the case of job portals.

Besides direct hiring, a social networking forum allows recruiters to prepare a talent pool for the future by interacting with candidates, engaging with them by means of polls, videos, company information, quizzes and so on. A company manages to not only create a community for its future hiring needs but also gets to crowdsource ideas for other needs.

Most companies want good talent, irrespective of the geographic location the talent comes from. Social networking portals are global in nature, and they have profiles of people from all geographies. Job portals are country specific, which in a way limits their usage by large companies.

The biggest advantage of social networking sites is that they allow you to build relationships.

Networking is an essential skill for getting a job. We cover networking and building of long-lasting relationships in a later chapter. Here our focus is on telling you how to use social and professional networking sites to find jobs. The best thing about networking sites is that they provide you with the means to market and brand yourself without being viewed as a job seeker!

Personal Branding for Job Seekers

One of the ways to know your brand value is to Google search yourself. Are you searchable? A quick search of your name shows how visible your brand is to search engines. If your profile does not show up in search results, you will need to work hard on this. You must consider adding SEO (search engine optimization) friendly keywords.

The first step and the key to marketing yourself is to make your profile stand out, like a brand. Personal branding is your story, and it must be like that of a brand; it must be consistent, reach the right people and make the desired impact. Your personal brand is a result of your strengths, your reputation, the trust you build and communicate and the unique attributes that you possess. Branding plays an important role in landing you a job and boosting your career. A strong personal brand can be established with regular, incremental and credible steps.

Choose a Social Media Platform and Ensure Consistency in Engagement

Build a good social media profile for yourself, using the same name, and maintain fully updated profiles on LinkedIn, Facebook and Twitter, ensuring that each profile is consistent in terms of colour and tagline. Also, make sure that your profile is in line with your objectives so that you are easily searchable.

Clean your profile: If your profile on professional networking sites has any inappropriate photos or content, then you should immediately delete them. If you want to keep your accounts for personal use, ensure that you turn on the private mode.

Develop a frequency and a niche to show authority: You should develop a pattern of engagement and post regularly, maybe on a particular day of the week (Tuesday morning is ideal, as on Mondays the work week has only begun for people, and they are likely to turn to social media only the next day. This has been our personal experience too). Start with LinkedIn and gradually increase your presence on Facebook and Twitter. Analyse your posts and identify an engagement pattern that works for you. Initially, you can try a niche area on which to post, to test the waters. You will slowly identify the areas that have a high degree of engagement. The more unique and engaging the content you post on your chosen topic of expertise, the more it will attract attention and establish you as original and effective among the key people whom you are targeting. However, always remember that your niche should be related to your targeted job area.

Network and engage with relevant people: Focus on engaging with relevant people who have been identified by you and who can be of help to you in achieving your career objectives. Be focused and nurture each relationship. Be specific, display depth and command in your chosen area and avoid run-of-the-mill statements. Posting views, articles and opinions which establish you as a thought leader or deep thinker will stand you apart from others.

Find, join and engage with groups: LinkedIn and Facebook offer millions of opportunities to choose a relevant group for yourself. Choose a group which has your targeted companies and people. Use these groups to find new opportunities, engage with people, show your authority and enhance your brand image.

Spend quality time regularly: Personal branding takes time and effort to develop. Your personal branding will entail the promotion of your projects, work and experience. For example, if you are searching for a marketing job, using words or phrases such as 'storytelling', 'writer' or 'content specialist' can help consolidate your personal brand.

Think about impact and impression before you post: Think about the impact of your post before sharing it on social media. Avoid commenting or sharing content on politics, religion or other sensitive issues. Any such post may give you few immediate likes, but will create a long-term negative perception about you.

Stories are more impactful than data: Tell a story about your work, life or project and how it created an impact. For example, if you volunteered for an NGO, then instead of posting a photo, create a story about the event, mentioning what you did and how it helped others. Be professional and be careful not to share personal information or to overdo it. Posting inspirational quotes is good, but posting them with your photograph may give the impression that you are trying to market yourself rather than sharing the quote to inspire! Personal branding is most valued during the hiring process. You will find many people branding themselves as an under-40 award winner, digital evangelist, etc. You must align your skills and experience to build a unique personal story which should communicate the value you will bring to the company you are seeking to work with.

If a company shortlists four candidates after interviews, it means they all have been considered suitable for the role. Before making their final hiring decision, most recruiters search for information about the candidates on Google. They may find that one of them does not have a social media presence. Two shortlisted candidates have a social media presence but they have posted more about politics and religion, or have posted casual photographs of themselves partying with friends. The fourth candidate may have a professional presence on social media. Obviously, in spite of all four being found suitable in terms of their education and experience and the competencies required by the company, the fourth candidate will get selected.

Make your social media presence right and positive. Remember, you are creating a personal brand for an objective (which is job search) and not to become famous. Be authentic about what and who you are and keep it limited to your professional area only.

The profile requirements for each site are unique, so your profile too needs to be different on each site. Online platforms like LinkedIn, Facebook and Twitter are popular among job seekers and employers. LinkedIn and Facebook are the most valuable tools in your job search, and highly recommended over Twitter, Instagram and other such platforms. Twitter, Instagram and other sites are very useful for finding out more about your prospective connections and to build long-term relationships with them. But, for direct job search or for getting discovered by companies, we recommend LinkedIn and Facebook.

LinkedIn

It is estimated that 87 per cent of recruiters use LinkedIn as part of their candidate search and this is reason enough for you to actively use it for job search. This provides you a platform on which to showcase your profile, your expertise, recommendations and connections. You can use it to not only create the best first professional impression when recruiters and employers use LinkedIn to search for candidates, but to also demonstrate your credibility in your industry and highlight your achievements.

Please use the following focused techniques on LinkedIn:

1. **Build a targeted network with the right people in the companies and industry where you are looking for a job:** It is important to send connection invites as per your job search strategy. Do not get lost in accepting or inviting everyone. Connect with people who you think can play a role in helping you achieve your objective of job search or for providing a reference. If you are not focused, you will be endlessly wasting time, like most people, without the desired outcomes.

2. **Write personalized and appealing messages to get your connection requests accepted:** While sending invitations, it is important that you write personalized, appealing and customized messages compelling the person to accept your connection or friend request. Address them by name/sir/madam to make the person feel that you are keen to connect with them and are sending a message customized just for them. It goes without saying

that you should proofread all messages before sending them! All professional networking portals prompt you with pre-written text messages. Please do not use them. Often, an invite carrying a pre-written text message from the portal will get rejected.

3. **Use the Advanced Search options:** It is important to explore and make use of all the features built into the LinkedIn platform. Use the LinkedIn search bar to find companies and professional groups that interest you, and 'follow' or 'join' these communities. The primary advantage is that once you have 'joined' a group, other members of the group who must be working in those companies you have targeted will be more open to being contacted by individuals from within the group.

4. **Use the 'Career Interests' segment effectively:** You should update the 'Career Interests' segment, which is available in the 'profile' section of LinkedIn. Toggle on the 'Let your recruiter know that you are open' tool and make it active. This will make your profile more searchable by the recruiter. If you are currently working somewhere, you should not worry. LinkedIn hides your job search preferences from recruiters and from anyone working in your current company or its associate companies.

5. **Use the 'Job' section and turn on the 'Job Alert' notification:** LinkedIn also has a 'Job' section where you can search for jobs in specific companies. If you are an active job seeker, then you should set your job alert based on what you are looking for and your location preferences. The job alert can be activated with search criteria like

'Location', 'Role', 'Experience Level' and 'Companies'. This will enable you to receive job notifications daily or weekly in your mailbox.

6. **Follow the target companies and people in your sector:** Follow companies and people who are working in the area of competence/companies/locations where you are looking for job. This will enable you to get immediately notified of any vacancy posted by these companies.

7. **Join alumni and professional groups:** Known people, people with common interests, or people in a group who are familiar with each other are more likely to help you. One of the best and easiest ways to leverage the power of LinkedIn is through using the Alumni tool. You can first join your college alumni group. You should also join the corporate alumni groups of companies where you have previously worked.

8. **Never say you are looking for a job:** Avoid writing 'job seeker', 'in transition mode', 'looking for challenging opportunity' or anything like that in your headline or while sending connection requests. This looks desperate, and people tend to avoid such requests. This is not because they do not want to help, but because they genuinely cannot help so many people.

9. **Use the Easy Apply feature:** The Easy Apply feature helps you apply for jobs with just a few clicks, saving you lots of time.

LinkedIn is a must platform for all professionals and job seekers.

Using Facebook for Job Search

Facebook has always been a great place to connect with family and friends. In 2017, it opened up its job feature, which is now widely used by recruiters and job seekers. If you are using Facebook for professional and job search purposes, the first thing you should do is to clean your pages of inappropriate photos or comments that you may have posted earlier, when you were less concerned about your 'professional online presence'.

1. **Review your Facebook page settings:** You can change privacy settings by clicking on the question mark icon on the top right of your screen. When you scroll down, you will find the option for 'Privacy'. Click on it and another menu bar will open, offering you the options below as well as more help with privacy settings. Click on each topic to see how Facebook shares information and how you can adjust your privacy options.

2. **Make the relevant section of your profile public:** It is advisable to keep most of your Facebook profile restricted to friends and family. However, some part of it should be viewable by the public if you are searching for a job. Keep your main photo public, along with your employment and educational details so that recruiters can view and find you.

3. **Complete your profile on Facebook:** If you want people to find your profile on Facebook, one way to enhance your profile is to add your past work history and professional skills to your 'About' section. Just click on 'edit profile',

and the top of the screen lists 'Work and Education'. If you want to make yourself known to the 65 per cent of recruiters who trawl for job candidates on Facebook, take a few minutes to fill out this information. You can even cut and paste from your LinkedIn profile, though we would suggest a shorter version for Facebook. It is a good idea to see what your public profile looks like when someone you don't know views it. Click on the three dots after 'View Activity Log' on your profile to select the public view. This only works from the desktop version of Facebook, not your mobile device as of now. You can use this feature to make part or the whole of your profile public.

4. **Create a Professional/Job category from your friends list:** Go to your list of friends and hover your cursor over the 'Friends' rectangle next to a professional contact's name. You'll see a roster of lists, including the option 'new list'. Create one called 'Professional' or 'Work' and then add to this list all the friends whom you would consider as professional contacts. This way, you can target your work-related status updates and send job-related information to this group of friends who can be of help to you.

You also do not want your family and other casual posts to seen by this professional group. So, while posting a status update, click on the rectangle that says 'Public' to the left of the word 'Post'. You'll see a pull-down menu that includes the word 'Custom'. Click on that and you'll see an option that says 'don't share this with', where you can type in 'Professional/Work'. This will ensure that your post will not be viewed by the 'Professional/Work' friends list.

5. **Make 'Friends' with the right people:** Refer to your career options and the key people list you have prepared for your job search purposes. Please send 'Friend' requests to them. Start with a few people from the list. Some will accept, some may not. When some of them who are in senior positions have accepted your requests, send your remaining 'Friend' requests. Now the chances of those requests being accepted are higher, because people generally refer to the 'you are also friends with' option before accepting requests. Keep this list growing regularly and consistently.

6. **Follow your target company and your interest groups:** Just like LinkedIn, Facebook too can link you to potential connections through its Groups feature. You can find groups of your interest by searching against keywords such as 'human resources' or 'marketing' in the search box. Follow the pages of companies in your target list. Though companies use Facebook to promote their products and services, and to post videos and news about themselves, their pages allow you to interact with other company fans and customers. As jobs get posted on company Facebook pages, don't overlook this potential source of opportunities.

7. **Be regular using 'Like' and 'Comment' with respect to your target companies:** 'Like' or 'Comment' when it comes to posts by companies in which you are looking for a job. Join their group, if it is open to all. By doing

this you can get daily updates about activities on their pages, which may include job-opening alerts.

8. **Search out jobs and start applying:** Facebook job postings can be found in two places:

   1. On companies' Facebook pages, under the Jobs tab.
   2. On the Jobs page, where you can use search to access job listings by location, industry, skill and job type.

You can click 'Jobs' in the left column of News Feed. In 'Jobs' on Facebook, you can search for jobs, change your location or select an industry or job type. You can also click 'Subscribe' in the right column to get notified about new job openings.

9. **Choose Facebook friends wisely:** Your friends' posts will be visible on your timeline. Inappropriate posts by your friends may reflect the company you keep, and any recruiters can also see your friends while visiting your profile.

10. **Use the 'Messaging' feature to strengthen relationships:** You can 'message' a good article, video link, or a photo to your targeted people to share something interesting with them and strengthen your relationship with them.

It may also be a good idea to join specific industry community forums to showcase your work, such as GitHub for developers, Flickr for photographers, Behance for artists, and Medium for writers. As and when required, you can share your work, along with the links, with these communities to establish your credibility.

Using Twitter for Job Search:

Each social media mode works differently and serves a different purpose. At first, you may notice that people only post on Twitter and most people do not read messages of others except the tweets of influencers and popular names. Since your objective is job search, it is also important to be there on Twitter and use it to your advantage.

1. **Act like a thought leader:** While LinkedIn is a great place to show off your professional experience, Twitter is a great place to establish yourself as a thought leader in your area. So, focus less on your personal accomplishments and more on sharing great articles related to your field, commenting on news in your industry and having conversations with key people.

2. **Follow your target company, recruiter and key influencers:** Follow companies and people in those companies where you are looking for a job. The good aspect of Twitter (unlike Facebook or LinkedIn) is that you can follow anyone and you do not need their acceptance to do so. If you do not know where and how to start, then use either Google to find key people's Twitter handles or go to Twitter directly and start following the key people you have identified. Twitter has a 'following' feature. You can go to the Twitter account of any person, click on 'follow' and connect with them instantly.

3. **Show your personality by expressing yourself creatively:** The real-time nature of Twitter is such that opportunities come and go at a rapid speed, so you need

to be signed in often, reading, liking, retweeting and commenting on posts or developments, and displaying your professional value. Stay away from political, religious, and other controversial posts or comments, even if you feel strongly about these issues. Remember your purpose of being there.

4. **Use your real name and information:** While many use fancy names for their Twitter handles, we recommend that you use your real name for your Twitter account, along with a brief biodata reflecting the type of work you seek. This will help recruiters find you. Unlike LinkedIn, where formality rules, you can be a bit more personal and creative on Twitter.

5. **Engage to impress:** Always like and retweet posts by people from your list whom you are following for job search purposes. Comment, reply with good insight, and add value to their tweets. When something strikes you as useful, funny or shareable, you can repost it. Since anyone following you may read what you post, maintain an upbeat, professional tone and gear your posts to topics that are aligned with your industry or field. Try not to overdo the use of links or rely heavily on reposts or retweets, as doing so does not show you to be a good conversational partner.

6. **Use the hashtag search function:** An important feature in both Facebook and Twitter is the use of hashtags to mark the subjects you are tweeting about, so that others who have that topic in mind can find like-minded followers among the users. Try #jobsearch, #jobpostings, #jobhunt, #employment, #recruiters,

#careers, #careerinIndia, #onlinejob or similar hashtags to locate jobs or people who may be currently seeking you for their companies. Companies post over a million opportunities monthly, helping them boost their brand visibility by integrating the posts with their ATS.

7. **Use keywords in your résumé/profile:** Most of the portals use high-end algorithms to identify keywords as per the job description in the profiles available on social media and find the profiles that match best. If you use the right keywords in your résumé and profile and use hashtags in your posts, then it is more likely that you will feature in recruiters' search results.

8. **Be apolitical and non-controversial:** You may have your opinions on religion and politics, as well as strong likes and dislikes. But since your objective is job search, it is important that you do not post anything related to anything controversial or which gives others a negative perception of yourself.

9. **Participate in tweet chats:** Follow tweet chats organized by your target companies and influencers/key people on subjects, areas or sectors of your job search and participate with positive and constructive inputs. Tweet chats by your targeted people are a good platform on which to catch their attention.

It is important to test different approaches and measure the results. It will not be easy to reach your goal without the three key pillars of planning: strategy, implementation and review of actions taken.

Finally, there is nothing that can replace personal connect. You should use social media to contact people and try to meet key connects over coffee or tea to make lasting relationships that will be beneficial to you for life.

Key Takeaways

1. Complete your profile and make relevant profiles for job search on social networking sites.
2. Optimize your presence on LinkedIn and use its features for faster job search.
3. Facebook also helps you search for jobs, in addition to connecting you socially. Use its Group and Job Search features (by location, job type) to find jobs near you.
4. Follow key people who are not accepting your requests on LinkedIn, Facebook, to build credibility with them so that you can approach them later.

Exercise

1. Use Advanced Search, Job Options, join Career Interest sections, alumni/company groups on LinkedIn and other social media platforms.
2. Work on Facebook settings, create your profile, categorize your friends' lists, join Job Group and search for jobs based on your preferences.
3. Use Twitter to follow key people who are important for your job search (who may not be accepting your connection/friend requests on LinkedIn and Facebook).

4. Do professional postings on all three platforms at least once a week.

Useful Free Sites/Groups

1. To find new people to follow, you can explore the following:

   a. twellow.com
   b. wefollow.com
   c. tweepz.com

2. LinkedIn Groups: There are many groups on LinkedIn for job search based on company, sector and role. I recommend that you join groups such as:

   a. **LinkedinHR:** A group of headhunters, recruiters and managers. It claims to be the biggest HR group on LinkedIn and its members are very active in supporting each other.
   b. **JobAlert:** This group is especially beneficial for middle- and senior-level management professionals looking for jobs in India, the United Kingdom and the United States of America.

6

How to Make Attractive Profiles on LinkedIn to Get Discovered by Companies

LinkedIn is an excellent platform for job search and networking. In this respect, it is much better than other networking sites. About 98 per cent of recruiters and 85 per cent of hiring managers use LinkedIn to find candidates. Approximately 87 per cent of recruiters use LinkedIn as part of their candidate search. More than 30 lakh companies from all around the world have official LinkedIn company pages, which you can visit to know more about them and the job vacancies posted by them.*

As a professional or a student, it is the best and most popular place to network and look for job opportunities. If you want to choose one social media platform for searching for a job, it has to be LinkedIn. Your powerful presence on

---

* Source: LinkedIn | Career Centre (utoronto.ca).

LinkedIn—coupled with the right strategy and use of its different features—can do miracles for your career.

A presence on LinkedIn can not only help you find a job directly with the company you have in mind, but can also help you connect with the right people in the industry of your choice, and build your own brand and rank on Google. This works both ways, you can find a job and also help recruiters find you. Making a great profile is the first step towards your objective.

1. Get a custom URL for your name

It is easier to share and publicize your profile using a customized URL (LinkedIn.com/yourname) than a complicated-looking combination of numbers that LinkedIn automatically assigns when you make your profile. This is very easy to get and simple to use. To get a customized URL:

- Go to the 'Profile' section
- On the top right-hand corner, click on 'Edit public profile & URL'
- Click 'Edit' and write your name or the URL you want and click 'Save'.

Now, if your name is Subir Verma, your URL will be https://www.linkedin.com/in/subirverma/ in place of the earlier https://www.linkedin.com/in/https://www.linkedin.com/in/subir-verma-0b918253/. This looks professional and makes it easier for recruiters and companies to discover you. It also looks cleaner in your signature when you are sharing your URL with others.

2. Choose a professional photo and background picture

The first thing that encourages other people to read, or open your request or profile, is your photo. Recruiters spend almost a fifth of their time looking at photos when reviewing LinkedIn profiles. Instead of a passport-sized serious-looking school ID card-type or casual hunk or funky-type photo, choose a clear, friendly, recent, smiling and professional image as your profile picture. You can use a casual picture on other social media sites like Facebook or Instagram. But, on LinkedIn, it has to be a professional photograph. Use a recent photo which actually indicates how you look in real life. It should be a close-up of a smiling face. The picture should be of high resolution (400x400 pixels), the face filling about 60 per cent of the space, with a simple background. You must have a smiling expression, and you must be in formal dress. You can use www.photofeeler.com or similar sites for knowing the quality, pixels and dimensions of your photograph before using it. A good profile picture will go a long way in conveying your passion, energy and charisma; qualities that cannot be conveyed through writing. It has also been observed that some people just connect with a photo for emotional reasons and go out of their way to extend support.

A background photo at the top of your profile page is useful to showcase yourself. It will engage visitors by grabbing their attention, and it also increases your profile's recall value. You can also use this space to showcase your achievements. You can use a photo showing yourself receiving an award, certificate, recognition, etc.

3. Write a short, specific and relevant headline

The headline of your LinkedIn profile is important, as it communicates your first impression to your prospective employer. When you send a connection request, the other person takes just a few seconds to decide to accept or reject you. Most people do not even open your profile to see it fully before deciding to accept or reject your request. Most decide to open your request based on the impression your photo and headline creates in their minds. The headline also plays an important role in getting your profile discovered by recruiters. A general practice is to write what you do (job title) and the name of the company where you work. But, if your designation is generic, it may not communicate what you do or indicate why a visitor should read your profile. It is recommended that you mention your industry, your functional expertise, and the key points that you think your target companies would like to know about you. You must use space to showcase your speciality, value proposition or uniqueness. You should add keywords and phrases, which can help a recruiter find you easily.

For example, Rakesh Das is currently working as Manager (Audit). He should not write 'Manager (Finance), ABC Company'. This headline does not communicate his qualifications, experience and skills. We recommend he write 'CA, CFE | 4+ years | Internal Audit, Risk & Control | Data Analytics | Power BI, Tableau'. Such a description communicates his qualifications, years of experience, certification and skills. This also has the keywords 'Power BI',

'Tableau' and 'Internal Audit', which will help him in being discovered by recruiters easily.

Please avoid writing 'looking for job', 'need change', 'searching for new challenges', etc. LinkedIn has millions of job aspirants. People tend to help those who have built credibility or relationships with them over a period of time.

4. The summary should showcase all of your professional work, skills and abilities

Your summary should be like a story through which a reader can know all about your qualifications, experience, skills, passion, industries, roles and, above all, the things that set you apart. People do not have the time to read too much; hence, it is recommended that you write two or three short paragraphs, with the key highlights as bullet points. You should write about the work you are doing in your current company, your contribution, key achievements and key skills. If you are a fresher, you must mention your projects, internships and other work done, which reflect the skills needed by your target companies. The summary should be the best personal marketing script for yourself. If you are not able to write your own script, then refer to the profiles of a few people who have the same background as you. You can prepare a customized script for yourself and use it. If you stay in a small city, you should write the name of the nearest metro or bigger city to help recruiters find you.

All social media sites are algorithm-driven, and it is important to include keywords in each section. This will help you to feature in the results when someone searches for candidates with your profile.

5. Use media, video, case study, link, to highlight your achievements

In 'Features', 'Experience' and other sections, you should attach pictures of your awards, videos, articles, talks, case studies, and other achievements, highlighting them to make a positive impression of yourself to the visitor browsing your profile. All this quickly establishes your credibility with your audience and impresses them.

6. Highlight your work, roles and achievements (filling all gaps) in the Experience section

List your current and previous experiences to highlight your work experience. You should also add details of your key role and achievements in each of your stints at every company you have worked for, along with links to the companies' websites. Write in simple, easy-to-read, short sentences. Use asterisks or plus signs to make a bulleted list. Focus on the benefits of your experience and achievements to keep readers engaged. If the companies where you have worked are not well known, then you should add brief information about them. If there is a gap between jobs, then write about the work, course, project or other activity you pursued during that time. If you are experienced at your job, then it is advisable to mention the certificates and awards, and attach videos and photos reflecting your experience and achievements at the companies you have worked in. This builds immediate credibility.

Your current company and work profile are very important, as companies search for profiles based on current job roles/company of employment. If you are a fresher or unemployed, your title can include the job title you are targeting. e.g., 'Full-time BE student/Social Media Marketer in Training'—followed by 'In Transition' in the Company Name box.

7. Impress with details about your education, projects, volunteer work and the languages you know

Each section of your LinkedIn profile is important and should be completed in such a manner that it communicates all you have done. In your physical absence, it is good to over-communicate. Write about all your projects, your success stories, the skills you possess, and the languages you speak, to make yourself stand out in the crowd and impress your prospective employer.

8. Showcase your achievements—professional, social and personal

When recruiters spend hours searching for high performers on LinkedIn, there is little to differentiate among profiles. Your professional, social and personal achievements become the key differentiators then, as they reflect the many values and attributes which companies may be looking for. Use action verbs to write about your promotions, key projects you have done, your social work, etc. For example, 'I got two consecutive promotions in two years', 'worked with NGO to extend support to daily wage earners by distributing food for ten days during the COVID-19 pandemic in 2021', etc.

9. Get recommendations to show on your profile

Recommendations are an endorsement of your good work by someone you have worked with. This is a great testimonial and is valued a lot by recruiters, especially if written by people who are authorities in their fields and have high credibility.

You should choose to show recommendations that are well written and relevant to your professional success. When you ask for recommendations, they are usually written using generic words, with no mention of your specific work or attributes. You can choose to request them to write again or dismiss them or simply let them be in 'pending' status. You should choose to show only those recommendations that are right for you. The rest you can 'Hide' or request for revision.

You should also keep adding to the recommendations. You should often visit your connects and request recommendations from seniors, colleagues and team members with whom you have worked or are working. Try to seek specific recommendations rather than generic-sounding ones. For example, 'Ramesh's contribution to project Muskurati Jindagi helped in increasing internal employee engagement by 5 per cent and also generated positive feedback from employees and their family members, specially kids', is better than 'Ramesh was a pleasure to work with, a great colleague, he will be an asset to any company and I wish him all success in the future'.

10. Focus on your skills and endorsements

The first step is to make a list of your relevant skills in your profile, based on your work experience and the job you are looking for. Endorsements are a great way to show off your skills and are given a lot of importance by recruiters. As you transition between careers or develop skills or take on new responsibilities, you should keep updating and adding to the list so that any visitor or connection viewing your profile can know about them.

11. Build the right connections, follow and join groups

People like to help those whom they know. Build connections and follow people based on your objectives. If your main objective is job search, then you should choose people based on what kind of jobs you are looking for, your target companies and your preferred job location, and build connections and relationships with them.

Never ask for a job in your connection request message or first few messages. If you do so, there are high chances that they may not even accept your connect request. Please remember, people receive many requests every day and it may not be possible for them to help everyone, even if they genuinely want to.

Join groups that will add value and contribute towards meeting your objective. You should join many relevant groups based on your career aspirations. You will find many key people on the platform and many vacancies posted by your desired companies. Also, follow a few relevant groups where you can build your credibility by being seen as a contributing member.

12. Contact information

If you are a job aspirant and want people to easily reach you, you should mention your contact details (mobile number and email ID). If you don't want to include your main email address for privacy reasons, you can set up a separate account earmarked for public sharing. But make sure that you check it regularly. It is good to share your other social media links, like your Twitter ID, for recruiters to know more about you.

13. Use of keywords and buzzwords

A keyword is a word or phrase used by people to search for specific information on web pages. It is part of a web page's metadata, and helps search engines match a page with an appropriate search query. You should use these keywords and buzzwords so that your profile can feature when recruiters search for profiles that match their needs. One of the best ways is to include the keywords, phrases and skills contained in the job description of your targeted roles. Let us take a brief example of a job posted on social media for 'marketing manager'. Generally, the job posted would contain the title of the position, qualifications, experience and skills required for the job; e.g., 'Looking for BE, MCA with MBA with 2 years of experience as Marketing Manager'. The role includes 'market research to uncover the viability of current and existing products/services', 'liaising with media organizations and advertising agencies', 'developing pricing strategy for product and services', 'business development', and 'achievement of revenue and sales targets'. The candidates must have 'excellent communication skills', 'knowledge of traditional and new-age channels', 'analytical skill to forecast', and 'influencing skill'. We advise you to use the exact key words as mentioned in the job description. This will help your profile appear in search results as and when any recruiter uses these key words.

14. Check your LinkedIn profile strength

LinkedIn is a powerful tool, which is easy to use and which provides you with a 'Profile Strength' feature to review your profile by optimizing it to grab attention, sell your skills and validate your accomplishments. There is a gauge on the right-hand side of your profile page that gives you a 'Profile Strength' measurement. Essentially, this tells you how complete your profile is. Keep adding more details to your profile, using the site's tips, until the gauge rates you as 'All-Star'.

15. Be polite and warm, but do not go overboard

You create a certain impression about yourself with your presence and posts on social media. Always be polite, warm and welcoming towards others. Since you are there for a purpose, be focused on conversing with people relevant to you and build relationships with them. When you post, share and like on social media, you must manage your presence in such a way that you are not viewed as someone desperate or going overboard for the sake of getting a job.

Finally, 'Be yourself, represent who you are.'

Create your LinkedIn profile keeping all these ideas in mind. Keep aside a few minutes every day to leverage LinkedIn and take advantage of its features and tools. You will be amazed what a difference it can make to your job search.

Key Takeaways

1. Build a complete profile and check 'Profile Strength'; work on your profile to make it 'All-Star'.
2. Use keywords in Summary, Title and other segments of your profile to get discovered.
3. Focus on building the right, quality and relevant connections.
4. Follow your target companies.
5. Join groups where your targeted people are present.
6. Contribute consistently.
7. Always be polite, respectful and warm.

Exercise

1. Complete your LinkedIn profile to show strength as 'All-Star'.
2. Join ten groups based on your targeted companies.
3. Build twenty connections every day with your targeted people during the first thirty days.

4. Create at least one post every alternate day.
5. Like, share and comment on posts by your targeted people every day.
6. Do not spend more than one hour every day on LinkedIn.

Useful Free Sites/Groups

1. **Join groups based on your location:** If you live in Mumbai, then join groups like 'Job Opportunities in Mumbai', 'Mumbai job opening'.
2. **Join groups based on your qualifications:** If you are an MBA and searching for jobs, then join groups like 'MBA job seekers group'—https://www.linkedin.com/groups/10442857/.
3. **Join groups based on the sector where are you looking for a job:** If you are looking for job in the services sector, then join groups like 'Job in Service Sector'—https://www.linkedin.com/groups/10406658/.
4. **Follow your targeted companies:** If you are ready with a list of your targeted companies where you would like to work, do follow them. If your target companies are Reliance Industries, Godrej, Tata Power, then visit the respective company pages:
   https://www.linkedin.com/company/reliance/,
   https://www.linkedin.com/company/godrej-group/,
   https://www.linkedin.com/company/tata-power/.
5. For profile picture photo quality, you can use www.photofeeler.com to check your photo for quality before using it.

7

How to Go about the Job Interview—
Before, During and After

You have most likely read many articles and watched many videos on how to give good interviews. But we are not going to talk about regular interview techniques as most job aspirants are already aware of them. Also, the techniques commonly recommended are, by now, well known and used by all. You need to know something that will make you stand out from others. We shall be sharing with you some practical insider tips.

It is important to mention that if you have been called for an interview, that means the selection has come down to the last four or five from an initial 100. This is your best opportunity to showcase your work experience, knowledge, skills and other qualities to prove that you are the perfect candidate for the job. But remember, the other candidates being interviewed for the job would also think along the same lines, would they not? Regular interview techniques, then, are not going to work! There is also a big chance that all the candidates will have similar qualifications, work experience and skills as you do. You need to find a way to stand out.

But how?

Focus on the Interviewer and Not on Yourself

Before we discuss this, let us re-emphasize the regular but important things you must do, before, during and after your interview.

Before interview:

- Plan your attire one day in advance.
- Dress formally and appropriately.
- Read the job description in advance.
- Prepare answers to frequently asked questions well.
- Practise your answers to frequently asked questions with a friend.
- Plan your schedule so that you can arrive ten to fifteen minutes early.
- Prepare a list of references.

During interview:

- Make the right first impression.
- Exhibit positive and good body language.
- Carry copies of your résumé, a notebook and pen.
- Treat everyone you encounter with respect.
- Win them over with your authenticity and positivity.
- Do not speak negatively about your previous employers.

After interview:

• Send a thank-you note to the interviewer.

If you are a serious job aspirant, you must follow these tips. In our view, these tips are usually followed by most job aspirants who attend interviews. We would say that these are basic requirements, the minimum you must take care to do. But they really do not make you stand out from the crowd or give you an edge in encouraging the interviewer to select you!

The word 'interview' is a combination of 'inter' and 'view', which means two or more people interact with and view each other to assess each other. Any job interview has two main goals: first, selection of the best candidates for the company, and second, selection by the best candidates of the company they want to join.

Every company has a job description (JD) for the role they are hiring for. The JD is a document that contains the educational qualifications, work experience, role and responsibilities, skill set, proficiency level and behavioural attributes required for the role. Interviewers assess each candidate against the requirements mentioned in the JD. This is an important document for both candidates as well as the interviewer. Generally, candidates either do not refer to the JD or do not give much importance to it. That is a mistake! The JD allows you to be focused. How much of what you know is important for the role? How much of what you have communicated with the company is really required by it? The JD allows you to take care of all this—just focus on what is required by the company instead of focusing on what you know.

In any interview, the focus of the interviewer is to assess you for the following and assess your suitability for the role for which they are hiring, as per the JD:

- Functional or technical knowledge
- Skills for implementing this knowledge at work
- Attitude
- Behavioural attributes required for the role
- Potential
- Cultural fit with the company

An interview does not happen in isolation but in an environment where there are more than two persons. The entire interview process involves more than just two or three persons. It involves the sourcing team, the recruiter, the hiring manager, the manager's boss, the HR manager/head, and sometimes members from the senior leadership team. They could be juniors, peers or seniors in the formal or informal hierarchy of the company. This group of people will decide whether or not you are the right fit for the job. The key to your selection rests with them. That is why you need to focus on them more than yourself.

You must use regular interview techniques, such as what to do before, during and after the interview, as mentioned in the beginning of this chapter. Since these are common techniques, as mentioned before, most candidates at an interview have prepared for it in a similar fashion. You need to present a different perspective to create a lasting impression so that you have an edge over the others.

Over the last two decades, we have noticed there are two facets to corporate hiring. One consists of published knowledge, what has been acknowledged and described in black and white; the other is the real and practical side. Based on the latter, and on our combined hiring experience of over thirty years, we have come up with additional techniques for approaching the interview, which we are sharing below. Learning them will help you emerge a winner.

1. Every company has two stories:
    a.   Company information, which is available to all.
    b.   Insider information, about people, culture and people practices.
2. Find out more about the role and the interviewer in advance.
3. Know your interviewer type and his/her expectations in advance.
4. Prepare anecdotes and stories in advance.
5. Score success in the first five minutes of the interview.
6. Think like an interviewer, not like a candidate.
7. Prepare for frequently asked questions and practise answering them.
8. Win over the interviewer even if you do not get the job.

1. Every company has two stories

It is a common and good practice to learn more about the company and role before going for an interview for a job there. An interviewer generally asks questions like, 'What do you know about the company?' or 'Why are you looking for a job in the company?' or 'How do you perceive the company in the industry?' or 'What are the competitive advantages the company has in the market?'. Knowledge of the company always helps. You can find out more about the company from its website, from visiting the company page on social media, the company annual reports, and many other sources.

All the above sources will give you lots of information about the company and maybe the role for which you are going too. The information will mainly be positive. It will not give you real insight or insider information about the company culture, its work environment, people practices and engagement. From the point of view of the interview, these things do not matter much as they will be important only after you join the company. Your purpose to appear for the interview is to get selected so that you have the option to join the company or not! It is important to find out more about the company so you can share your knowledge of it and impress your interviewers. Glassdoor is a good platform on which to get real insights into a company and feedback from people who have worked or are working there. Note down some positive points from there, which you can share during the interview. Share a few things that you have learnt that are not commonly known too. This will create a positive impression about you.

Connect with a few employees who have joined the company recently, preferably in the team for which you are being considered. How do you connect with them? Search for them on social media, on LinkedIn, Facebook and

Twitter. Tell them you are looking for guidance as you have an interview with the company where they are working. Try to get their phone numbers. Call them, or even better, meet them over a cup of tea. Learn more about the company from them.

Many aspects about the company are important. But there are two critical things which you must learn more about for meeting your objectives. They are: your role, and your interviewers.

2. Find out more about the role and the interviewer in advance

All companies have JDs for each role they want filled. The JDs specify functional and behavioural competencies (knowledge, skill and attitude) and the proficiency levels required for the job, and this is used by all interviewers to assess candidates during their interview to select the person best suited for the role. As interviewers are also human, they too have emotions and feelings, which play a significant role in the actual hiring decisions.

What answers you respond with and how the interviewers receive and understand them is more important than being correct. Although there are competency-based interviews that judge candidates for their knowledge, a typical interviewer will decide within the first few minutes whether he or she likes you or not, and this is likely to affect the outcome of the interview. It is very important to give a good impression to your interviewer from the very first moment you meet him or her. From the start of the interview, you must look at the signals being sent out in the questions that come your way, and decode the jargon to find out what actually the interviewer wants to hear. Use this approach to answer each question in the interview. You can use the following technique to answer each question:

- **L**isten to find out what competencies or attributes the interviewer is looking for.
- **O**bserve his or her body language, especially the eyes, to get signals during and after the questions he or she has asked.
- **F**rame and share relevant stories/practical work done by you that match the interviewer's expectations.
- **E**nhance or reduce the length and focus of your answers, based on the signals you are detecting.
- **R**emain focused more on the interviewer's body language signals than on your answers. Quickly identify signals and change track if the interviewer does not seem interested, by sharing additional experiences/examples, like project work, internship, volunteering, social work, working with different groups where collaboration or teamwork was involved.

If you do not have previous experience or do not remember work-related examples to share with the interviewer, please use a variety of examples from your personal life; you can talk about your volunteer work, hobbies, etc. This way, you are not only telling your interviewer/s about your professional accomplishments, but also giving them good insight into who you are as a person outside the workplace. Use a different story for each question. Each interviewer will see the same questions and answers differently. Expectations of interviewers differ, depending on their personality type and experience they have. If three candidates meet the merit requirement of the role, then an introvert interviewer is more likely to select an introvert candidate from the three candidates.

What you actually did has no importance if it fails to meet the expectation of the interviewer.

An interview is a mechanism for selection of candidates for a job and is not about self-disclosure. Therefore, you do not need to unnecessarily extend information about yourself. Never respond by saying, 'I haven't done that before.' Think of something similar you have done and describe that. Be specific and give real-life examples while being honest. For example, if you are being asked to share an example of leadership, you can mention leading a project team or football team or a similar activity you have done. The response should be relevant and appealing to the interviewer. General or theoretical approaches won't fetch you marks.

We strongly recommend a structure, a framework, system or process which breaks the whole mechanism into parts and helps you develop a solution. This approach also helps you respond to most of the questions that come your way even if you do not have enough knowledge to answer them accurately. One such technique that I recommend for interviews is the STAR technique.

STAR is an acronym for Situation, Task, Action and Result. There are four steps in the STAR technique:

- Situation (setting the scene)
- Task (describing what you wanted to achieve)

- Action (communicating what you actually did)
- Result (how the situation was resolved)

It will be easier for you to respond to any question and have enough points to talk about if you break down any interview answer into these four sections.

Once you have decided to follow the above technique, practise it for some time to internalize it. Practise it aloud and rehearse for your interview.

The world's best speakers are the best because of two reasons; they prepare well before their speech and then practise a lot to make it look natural.

3. Know your interviewer type and his/her expectations in advance

Know as much as you can about the roles and the people in the hiring process. If you know your opponent well, it will be easier for you to play your game as per your strengths and win. It is important to be well prepared, but it is even more important to know the expectations of the interviewer and the company so that you can communicate exactly what they are looking for.

In addition to using various networking techniques, a simple way to figure all this out is to frequently connect with the person who is scheduling your interview.

If you get a call directly from the company, ask the recruiter about the interviewer. Remember, the recruiter's credibility is also at stake, along with yours; hence, the recruiter will be happy to share more information. Ask him or her about the role, the company, the expectations, the people who are involved in the hiring process, their likes and dislikes, and any other information that can give you insights to prepare your answers for the interview.

If you are going through a recruitment consultant, please ask for the same information. Both recruiter and consultant will be happy to gather this information for you. If you ask, they will share insider information and inputs that could be decisive nuggets for your preparation, allowing you to make a lasting impression at the interview.

Know the type of interviewer you are meeting

Every human has certain behavioural attributes—they may be introverted, extroverted, soft-spoken, aggressive, submissive, optimistic, pessimistic, trusting, etc. From the interview perspective, you should quickly find, by active listening and observation, the type of interviewer you are faced with. There are many theories about the different types of interviewers, classifying them as The Friendly, The Interrogator, The Rule Follower, The No Nonsense, The Intimidating One, The Busy Man, etc.

You should know something about the interviewer before your interview. Their social media presence and posts will clearly tell you what kind of interviewer he or she is going to be. If you cannot find this out through social media, then you need to rely on the information you get from the recruiter or the consultant, or you can try to know the interviewer in the first five minutes of your interaction with the person.

Based on our three decades of hiring experience, hiring thousands of candidates and interacting with many interviewers, we find only two types of interviewers:

1. Those who prefer you to be in focus.
2. Those who prefer themselves to be in focus.

1. How to know the 'Prefer-you-to-be-in-focus' interviewer:
   Dos and don'ts with this type:
   A prefer-you-to-be-in-focus interviewer expects you to speak. Such an interviewer follows the traditional interview protocol and asks short questions and appears to be straight-faced and less emotional. He or she asks more subjective questions, looks keenly at you, and does not waste their or your time. For the entire duration of the interview, this type of interviewer encourages you to speak and tries to get as much as possible from you before making his or her decision.

   If you meet this type of interviewer, you should be prepared for lots of questions. Do not expect to receive helpful feedback to gauge how you are doing. His or her every question is for a purpose and to evaluate you. Listen to such an interviewer carefully and answer the questions with composure and in detail. Share your past work, accomplishments and data. Do not analyse the situation too much. Do not be in a hurry to answer; take your time, and think before answering. Such an interviewer is a blessing, as you get lots of time to talk about yourself. You can expect an unbiased evaluation from such an interviewer.

However, this kind of interviewer is boring, as the interview will be mostly one-way. Avoid telling stories about your personal life, parties and hobbies that are not relevant. They will not interest him or her. If you are not sure about the answer to a question, say so. Such an interviewer may ask 'wrong' questions to test your abilities and character. He wants insight into your skills and personality.

2. How to know the 'Prefer-themselves-to-be-in-focus' interviewer:

Dos and don'ts with this type:

'Prefer-themselves-to-be-in-focus' interviewers are self-obsessed and keen to share their own achievements, work and personal stories. They are talkative and have a good sense of humour, often making sarcastic comments. They are full of energy and impatient at the same time. They expect that you should know about them, their work and the contribution they have made to the company and to the lives of others!

If you meet this type of interviewer, then you should always keep your focus on them. They expect you to say good things about them, boost their ego, praise and behave like a commoner in a king's hall. You need to continually (without crossing the limit) flatter them, talking about the kind of work they have done, their contribution to the company, their influencing posts and inspiring blogs on social media, etc. If you have read their work, articles or social media posts, do not miss the chance to praise them and say how much you liked the posts and how much they impacted you. Just play along and do not disturb the moment. While you need to answer professionally, you also need to keep them at the centre.

With such an interviewer, avoid praising anyone else too much. Stay in your comfort zone. Just because this interviewer is ready to cry on your shoulder or is sharing all his stories, including jokes and personal matters, do not feel pressured to share such things from your side too. Try to steer the conversation back to the job and to how suitable you are for the job. Avoid taking a position with your answers or being adamant, even if you are right. Politely make your point and leave the judgement to the interviewer.

4. Prepare anecdotes and stories in advance

People forget numbers and pictures but remember stories. From our childhood onwards, we all gather stories in our lives—experiences that reflect our various qualities, attributes and outcomes. Remember those stories from your childhood, school and college days and work life, and prepare five to ten of them in response to the key types of questions you expect to be asked. Rehearse them and make sure they really get across the positive impact you have made in many situations, resulting in positive outcomes.

You can follow four steps to prepare your **BEST** story:

- **B**ackground and foundation-laying to grab attention
- **E**stablishing characters and options

- **S**olutions to the problems in question
- **T**urning point, with the outcome that projects your attributes

Your stories will not only make you different from other candidates but also create a wow impression. You must prepare impactful stories for questions that are frequently asked in interviews.

'Tell me something about yourself.'

Almost every interview starts with this question, and for almost all candidates this is a lost opportunity, because they respond by beginning with telling their name, describing their family background, education, job history, projects and hobbies. This is not only a waste of a golden opportunity but also creates a boring impression because you are saying what is already written in your résumé. Instead, use this question as an opportunity to tell a short but memorable story about yourself. A story that explains, heart-to-heart, why you are the most suitable person for the job.

Understand why that question is being asked. 'Tell me something about yourself' is being asked to make you comfortable and because they also want to know who you are (beyond what is written in your résumé), what you have done, your personality traits, and what you want in life. This question is like a free hit in a cricket match! Use this to tell an impactful (and well-prepared and practised) story to connect with the interviewers and leave a lasting impact on them.

Pick the relevant stories from the four or five that you have prepared already. Your story should be relevant to the context. Include something about the obstacles that you overcame as a result of your character or qualities that the interviewer is looking for. The story should be short and take not more than two minutes to tell. This should be practised. But you should not show yourself as a superhero, as the Hulk of the Avengers.

Here's an example.

Debashish is being interviewed for a manager sales role for a software solutions company which targets large companies as its customers.

His story in response to 'Tell me something about yourself' should be something like this:

'Five years back, I started working as a software developer among a group of eighty in a remote development centre. We developers created an innovative piece of software, but the sales team was too busy to give us any priority as they were busy with their work.

'I was scared to get away from my computer screen. But the goal of making the software successful inspired me. I volunteered to call up a few big customers to discuss and showcase the software that we as a team had developed. We went to a few customers and demonstrated how the software could solve real-life problems for them. After a few rejections, we entered into a deal with a big corporate house, as they realized that the software was going to save them fifty lakh rupees a year.

'The client bought our software and gave an advance to further customize it to their needs.

'It was at that point that I realized that I loved selling and solving problems for customers more than I loved coding.

'And I have been in sales ever since!'

The above story tells far more about Debashish's entrepreneurial attitude than the standard response most candidates in his position would make. The interviewers now know about his rising to the need of his company, showing problem-solving skills, being a team player and supporting his company unasked.

Stories are powerful tools of communication. They can set you ahead of the competition. There are some common areas around which you can build your stories:

a. *Stories about change:* Every interviewer wants to know how you adapted, managed and responded to change. Keep a compelling story ready.
b. *Where you see yourself in the next five years:* Use this story to communicate how focused you are, starting from your current situation to sharing your vision for the future.
c. *Your strengths and weaknesses*: Focus on one or two specific strengths relevant for the job. Quality is more important than quantity in your story, to effectively communicate your message.
d. *Why you want to work for this company or why you should be hired by it*: There can be no better opportunity than this to sell yourself. The interviewer wants to know how

much you know about the company and its culture and the role you are applying for. You have to use this opportunity to highlight the qualities that generally make you stand out. In your story, please add unique points about the company, including its culture and the future opportunities that it offers. Don't forget to mention how you can contribute to the company.

e. *A time or situation when you failed*: The story need not include a long list of weaknesses you have. Instead, focus on one area you are working on and in which you have made some progress. For example, presentation skills, public speaking or collaboration skills.

f. *Why you are leaving your current job*: The interviewer is looking for evidence of issues you might be facing in your current company. Always treat your current company and its people with respect, despite the myriad differences you may have with them. Never criticize your past and current employers, not even behind their back. In your story, please focus on your strengths, for example, how you resolve conflict. Also, mention how you aspire to learn new skills and grow in the new company.

Stories help you to be different from the rest and create a lasting impression. Prepare as many stories as you can and use them at the right time. However, do not overdo it.

5. Score success in the first five minutes

We interacted with more than 400 interviewers for this book. Based on those interviews, research and our own experience of being in HR for more than three decades, we can confidently say this:

Most interviewers make up their mind about a candidate in the first five minutes of the interview, and the remaining time they spend validating their decision.

What should you do in the first five minutes?

First, introduce yourself with energy, enthusiasm and express your appreciation for their time. Start off by saying, 'I had really been looking forward to meeting you (do not use the word 'interview'). The company is doing so well with some great products (or services), and leaders like you contributed immensely to its success. I am really looking forward to being part of this great journey.'

Make a customized introduction for the company and prepare this first introduction

If you can find some personal attributes/contributions/ interests of the interviewers, then add that appreciation; e.g., 'I am a big fan of your posts on LinkedIn and they really are a motivation for many people like me.'

You have to find ways to create this energy and interest within so that your interviewers find you different from the others. They will then be interested enough in you to invest their time in continuing the interview, giving you greater opportunity to prove your worth.

Remember, the introduction has to be more about the interviewer than about yourself.

6. Think like an interviewer, not like a candidate

All interviewers start with some doubt in mind about you, as all candidates are going to talk about themselves, their education, work experience and qualities. They all want to impress upon the interviewer their suitability for the job. However, the catch is, you do not know what the interviewer is looking for! Like you, the others too would have shared with the interviewer the good work done by them. What you have done and how much you have achieved is not important at all, but what the interviewer thinks about you is. In an interview, you should quickly be able to assess what the interviewer is looking for and align your answers to meet her expectations and create a positive impact. Positive body language, listening to the questions before answering, knowledge about the role and company, being respectful and enthusiastic, and a smiling face, are some key attributes you must display to create a good first impression in the first few minutes of an interview.

7. Prepare for frequently asked questions and practise answering them

Will it not be good if you know in advance the questions that your interviewers are going to ask you? Well, you can anticipate at least some of the questions, if not all of them. Yet, most candidates go for their interviews only half prepared.

In any interview, if there are twenty questions asked, you will find that 50 per cent of them are common and predictable, the answers to which can be prepared in advance. The most effective way to prepare for an interview is to prepare for these frequently asked questions and practise your response to them. You must prepare for the following frequently asked questions:

Questions about yourself:

- Tell me something about yourself.
- Where do you see yourself in five years?
- What are your strengths?
- What are your weaknesses?
- Why is there a gap in your education?
- Why do you change jobs so frequently?
- Please share some of your professional and personal achievements.
- What are the three things you have done in life that you are proud of?
- Narrate a situation where you exhibited leadership skills.
- Please tell me about a time and incident where you failed, and your learnings from that failure.
- How do you deal with pressure?
- If we call your current/previous manager/colleagues, how will they describe you?
- What did you do to improve your knowledge and skills in the last six months?
- What is your opinion about work-life balance?
- What motivates you in life?
- What are your hobbies and passions?

- Why did you leave your last job?
- What is your salary expectation?
- Are you willing to relocate?

Questions about the role and company:
- What do you know about the company?
- What are you looking for in a job?
- Why do you want to work for our company?
- What do you expect from your manager and team?
- What are the three things that are important to you in any job?
- Why should we hire you?
- Do you want to ask us any questions?

Prepare a script for each question, with the key points you want to highlight to the interviewer. Do not trust your memory, please write the points down. Revise and finalize your script for each question. It is useful to seek help and read your script to a few people you know for feedback. After you are satisfied with your script, practise by reading your responses out aloud rather than in your mind. As you speak out aloud, you will realize what direction you are going in; you will become aware of the pronunciation and impact of each word. Practise to the extent that you remember your responses in full. As you practise more, you will find yourself more confident and comfortable. One of the recommended ways to practise is to video-record your answers. Review the recordings and make improvements. Do this a few times till you are satisfied with your performance.

8. Win over the interviewer even if you do not get the job

If a salesman comes to you, gives an excellent demonstration of his product, then thanks you for your time and leaves without asking you to buy his product, would you buy from him? Not many would buy. Some customers take their own time to think about the purchase before arriving at a decision, don't they? The same happens in the case of job interviews too. It is always good to be in the good graces of people in the organization where you are looking for employment. You never know who may push your case. You must express your excitement and interest for the role and company. Do that before you walk out of the interview room.

'It was a pleasure to meet you and I am really excited about this role and company, and am looking forward to working with you and for the company [give some reasons based on your discussions at the interview and say that you look forward to their early feedback].'

This brings two advantages. One, if there are two equally good candidates at the end of the search, the interviewer is likely to think that you are more likely to accept the offer and will contribute more to the company. This may result in their making you the offer. Your thank-you and parting note should follow the **SKY** pattern:

a.   **S**how interest in the interview, job and company.
b.   **K**ey attributes are mentioned, as to why you are a good match for the company.
c.   **Y**ou disarm the interviewer and build a connect for a future relationship.

Two, even if you do not get the job, you will leave a mark. There is a higher probability of your getting referred in that company later or maybe even to another company by the interviewer.

Your interview is not over just because you walked out of the interview room. Most of the candidates look at the interview as a transactional relationship and forget the interviewer if they are not selected. With a likely average tenure of three years at a company, you will need to build relationships not only to seek support for the role for which you appeared in the interview now and but also for future roles. You should send a personalized thank-you email, mentioning a few key points and learnings and expressing your interest in working in the company and with the manager who interviewed you in the future. Keep the email short, to the point, personalized, respectful and error-free.

Here is a sample format for such a thank-you letter:

Subject: 'Thank you for your time'

Personalized greeting: Begin with a personalized 'Dear ABC Sir' or 'Hi, Mr Mathur'

Note of appreciation: Thank them for their time and express your appreciation for the way they interacted with you. Please mention the job title for which you were interviewed, as the interviewer may have met many candidates for multiple positions at once. For example, *'Thank you for taking the time to discuss the marketing manager position with me today.'* Next, write about something specific discussed at the interview that you enjoyed learning about or were impressed with, so that they know it is written just for them.

Recap of your qualifications: Reaffirm your experience and mention a few skills that you have, which are required for the role, and which should give them the confidence to select you. For example, *'My two years of experience in social media marketing and search engine marketing along with Google certification in the same area give me the confidence to excel in this marketing role.'*

Re-emphasize your interest in the role: Write how excited you will be to hear from them about the next step. It will be impressive if you can attach an article that would be of interest to them. For example, *'I am taking the liberty to share with you an excellent case study of Google published in Harvard Business Review, which you may like to read in your leisure time.'*

The way forward and contact information: In the end, thank them again and mention how eagerly you are looking forward to hearing from them. Don't forget to mention your contact details. If your social media pages are professional looking, you can add their links to your email signatures.

An interview should be your starting point in building your network. Keep in touch with the interviewer and nurture that relationship to gain benefits later in your career.

Key Takeaways

1. Acquire knowledge of the role and know the interviewer before you go for the interview.

2. Prepare your stories using the BEST method and practise telling them.
3. Score success in the first five minutes.
4. Use the STAR technique to answer questions.
5. Use a story to share your experience to stand out.
6. Keep in mind that the interview is more about the interviewer than about you.
7. Prepare for frequently asked questions.
8. Thank them using the SKY method to create a lasting impression.

Exercise

1. Write and practise telling ten stories using the BEST method from your personal and professional life that reflect your positive attributes.
2. Write and practise your interview introduction.
3. Write answers to frequently asked questions using the STAR technique and practise.
4. Write your thank-you script using the SKY method.

Useful Free Sites

1. **www.pramp.com:** This is a free portal for interview practice. You can book interview slots and practise for free, based on your qualifications, experience and the kind of job you are looking for. This also allows you to practise for both behavioural as well as technical interviews. Once you register, it blocks your calendar with probable questions, which allows you time to prepare before the

actual interview. You can also opt for a technical or coding interview for Java, C++, Python, PHP, etc., and can take as many practice interviews as you like for free.

2. **www.how2getjob.com**: This portal is all about how to get a job. It has end-to-end modules for students as well as for experienced job aspirants and covers sample answers to frequently asked questions.

8

Cracking the Campus Interview

More than 900 organizations hired more than 2,00,000 graduates from 4500+ colleges in India in 2020.[*] This is the best way for a student to get a good job. The final year of college is a very important period for any student. Every student aspires to get a great job and a great career opportunity before completing their course on campus. In the outside world, the job market is full of challenges and is marked by stiff competition. Hence, campus placements are among the most important events in any student's life. It is also a fact that only 10 per cent of students passing out of any course get jobs in campus recruitment drives. The rest—90 per cent—are either not placed or under-placed.

Getting hired at a company's campus programme is every college student's dream. The campus programmes of large companies, such as the 'Unilever Future Leadership Programme' of Unilever, 'Tata Administrative Services'

---

[*] Top 100 Engineering Colleges in India 2015 | siliconindia.

of the Tata Group, 'Godrej Laud' of Godrej, and other corporate hiring drives, have proved to be leadership factories for those companies.

Campus recruitment drives are the most sought-after hiring events among students. Campus recruitment is the process of hiring students directly from colleges and universities. It helps companies hire the best and the brightest of students straight off the campus. This is among the most preferred ways for a company to build its talent pipeline. Based on their industry niche, products and services offered, the market they operate in, and their culture and future business plans, each company has its own campus recruitment strategy. This strategy targets specific colleges, or targets programmes (BE, MBA, MCA, CA, CS, BA, BCom, etc.), and includes employer branding and continuous engagement with students, in order to attract the best and to generate interest among the student community in the company.

Due to the unemployment rates in the country, many experienced candidates are available at lower salaries than campus hires. But organizations prefer campus recruitment because there are many benefits to it:

1. Campus students are full of new ideas and perspectives and are also aspirational

Students are generally smart, creative and ambitious. They want to contribute, to make a mark and change the world fast. Unlike in the past, all companies need new ideas, innovation, out-of-the-box thinking and faster execution at the marketplace to stay ahead of the competition. Campus hires are a huge source of fresh knowledge; they bring new perspectives and different ways to deal with the challenges facing companies in the current times. As they are not exposed to the processes and culture of the company, they contribute a fresh perspective, fresh ideas and suggestions to the company, which could be game changers for it.

2. Students are more familiar with the latest trends, techniques and technologies

As they study current research models, theories, trends and technologies, it becomes very useful for companies to employ students and stay ahead of trends. Around the world, students have better ability, proficiency and acumen to follow and perform technology-related applications faster than the workforce of the previous generation.

3. Students are generally enthusiastic learners, adapt faster and are easier to manage

Being new to the company, students want to make their mark fast. They are eager to learn, to multitask, and are result-oriented, keen to prove themselves in the shortest possible time. It is easier to manage them as they see their managers as experienced mentors, and thus it is easier to mould and manage them, rather than someone who has worked elsewhere before.

4. Retention rates of campus hires are high, and they also work for lower salaries than more experienced hires

A campus hire has the best retention rate among all hires and is more loyal than later hires, given the right onboarding experience, role and support in the company. Campus hires feel it is their first job and that it will be the foundation for their learning and their future career. Often, students give more weightage to the company brand, the role, and the learning and growth opportunities they can get, than to just compensation. Above all, the compensation for campus hires will always be lower than for experienced later hires.

5. Employer-branding for life

Companies hire on campus not only to get good talent but also because it is a great opportunity for them to build their brand among young people. Even if the company does not hire many on campus, the students will remember the company as they continue on their career paths. The campus drive is not about hiring alone—most of the talented employees of tomorrow are also on campus right now. Students have large networks of alumni and friends and communicate a lot on social media. A company's presence on campus can not only help make an effective impact on students but also reach out to their networks.

We have seen many students who have been unemployed for many years. Recruiters have a perception that students who did not get a job in the passing-out year are simply not good enough. It is therefore very important for students to take campus recruitment seriously and prepare for it.

There are two types of campus recruitment drives you will come across—the **on-campus drive** and the **off-campus drive**. In on-campus placement, companies visit a college campus to recruit final-year students of that particular college for entry-level positions. Off-campus recruitment is conducted at a common place or college, or virtually, where students from different colleges participate in the placement drive. The off-campus drive is also referred to as 'pool campus'. The recruitment process followed by companies is almost similar, off-campus and on-campus, but the difference lies in the competition. In on-campus, you compete with your own college mates, whereas in off-campus, the competition will consist of students from other participating colleges also.

It is important for you to know the campus recruitment process and start preparing well in advance so that you are able to make the best impression and get the job you are eyeing. Generally, the campus selection process by any company consists of:

1. A pre-placement talk
2. Inviting of applications based on educational qualifications/eligibility
3. Written tests
   a. Aptitude test
   b. Technical/coding test
4. Group discussion
5. Technical interview
6. Panel and HR interviews

1. **The pre-placement talk**: This is a presentation given by the company, which includes information about its vision, mission, culture, business, achievements, the roles it wants to hire for, job locations, selection process,

learning and growth opportunities, and compensation and benefits. Companies generally inform colleges in advance of the proposed date for this pre-placement talk and invite students to attend. The objective of this talk is to create interest among the top students and invite them to attend the selection process of the company. Most companies hold their pre-placement talk and selection process on the same day to save time. Though the talk is a mass presentation, you are advised to take it seriously and make an impression at this stage by asking some relevant questions about the company, the growth opportunities there and related points. This you should prepare for before going for the talk.

2. **Inviting of applications based on education qualifications/eligibility:** In their pre-placement talk, the companies usually mention the minimum eligibility criteria for appearing for their selection process. The general qualification criteria for reputed large companies are based on one's grade, and scores in the 10th and 12th grades, and in BE/MCA/MTech/MBA courses.

3. **Written tests:** These make for the elimination round, and companies either conduct these tests themselves or through an assessment partner. In current times, most companies conduct computer-based written tests rather than pen-and-paper tests. Since this is the elimination round, it is very important that you take the tests seriously. You may be the best in your college, but if you are not able to clear these written tests, you will not get an interview opportunity. The written examinations are generally conducted to assess candidates for:

a. Aptitude
b. Technical/coding test

a. **Aptitude test:** This test is conducted by companies to measure your **capacity or ability to learn new things** if you are given adequate training. Companies conduct this test for freshers as they have had little or no work experience. The questions in this test will assess you for factors like numerical reasoning, verbal reasoning, abstract reasoning, speed, accuracy, consistency and problem-solving. Such a test contains objective-type questions, and if you prepare well in advance, you can crack it with ease. The aptitude test assesses a candidate for **numerical reasoning** based on statistics, charts, graphs and figures; for **verbal reasoning,** to ascertain if the candidate can comprehend complex concepts expressed in simple English; then are the **diagrammatic tests** to check for ability to analyse a sequence of inductive shapes, abstract patterns and sometimes numbers; the **situational judgement tests** to assess how you approach situations that you may encounter in a workplace; the **inductive reasoning tests,** to know how you make your decisions from certain observations; the **cognitive ability test,** which tests your mental activities, reasoning skills, understanding of situations, ability to remember a sequence of activities and solve puzzles; the **mechanical reasoning test,** which assesses your technical and engineering abilities; and the **in-tray exercises,** which test your ability to solve problems in business-related scenarios.

How to crack the aptitude test

Practise as many mock aptitude tests as you can before the campus event. The Internet is full of such tests, but you should focus on solving the practice tests set up by the company which is planning its campus recruitment. For example, if you want to sit for an aptitude test conducted by Amazon, then you should practise the aptitude tests conducted by Amazon during the last three or four years. The tests set by most companies will have questions to do with the number system, equations, ratio and proportion, percentages, profit and loss, time and work, time speed distance, areas and mensuration, averages, permutations and combinations, probability, plane geometry, seating arrangements, sets, progressions, functions, series, coding, and truth and lie-based puzzles.

Carry rough paper, a calculator (if allowed), pen, pencil, eraser and a watch to the test. While most aptitude questions are conducted online, you should use these to do your rough work for your answers. Questions with graphs, tables and pie charts are a little difficult.

Avoid spending too much time on one question if you are not sure about it. Move on to the next question. You must practise section-wise with a timer so that you are able to attempt most of the questions you know in time. Getting stuck on one question for too long may cost you your complete test.

Mark the unanswered questions and return to attempt these questions in the end. These tests also assess your time-management skills. Most of these tests have negative marking.

You should avoid making wild guesses; you should also avoid procrastination. Your aptitude test may score you for speed and accuracy. It's important that you do not guess haphazardly or hurriedly try to finish all the questions. Try to work as carefully as possible and at a decent speed. Allocate a fixed time to every question. So, play smart. After each practice session, analyse your answers and see where you went wrong.

The night before your aptitude test is important. Revise all your concepts and the important formulae of number systems, highest common factor, lowest common factor, time and work, averages, percentages, profit and loss, time and distance, thoroughly. Revise for two or three hours but do not overthink or worry. Sleep in time and for an adequate duration to feel fresh in the morning.

On the day of the actual test, do your best. Have confidence in yourself and avoid discussing the test with friends as it will put you under pressure, which may dent your self-confidence for the next round of the selection process.

b. **Technical/coding test:** This is another screening and evaluation process used by companies to shortlist the most relevant students from among thousands of technical candidates against pre-decided parameters. This test provides insights into the extent of knowledge students can apply and their basic understanding of technical matters. Some companies conduct a single technical test, while some, especially those hiring in the computer science domain, have two rounds.

The technical round is conducted by means of multiple-choice questions (MCQs). Core companies, for all branches of engineering or management, conduct technical tests to assess a candidate's essential knowledge, concepts and application, and ability at analysis for higher and future levels of thinking. Information technology companies conduct two rounds of technical tests—an MCQ test for technical abilities and then a coding test for the specific coding needs they require. The technical test is conducted to assess the candidates' grasp of the domain (programming knowledge and core skills), their capacity for practical application of their knowledge in real-life situations and their clarity of thought. Generally, there is no sectional cut-off, but there is an overall cut-off. Hence, you are advised to analyse your strengths and weakness and spend time on questions where you are confident of scoring the maximum marks in the least time and skip questions you are not sure about. Each company has different patterns of tests, based on their recruitment needs. You must practise the previous-year tests of the company whose tests you are going to appear for at the campus selection. There are many portals that offer practice papers for different sections; they are provided at the end of the chapter. There are many more available for free, which we highly recommend you use for practice.

4. **Group Discussion (GD): Debates, Discussions, Decisions**—these are the important 3 Ds of corporate

life. Debates and discussions are not only about making your point. They require many soft skills, which is what companies judge you on when they conduct the group discussion, an important part of campus recruitment. You will be judged for the following skills in a group discussion:

- How good and effective you are while communicating with others
- Your behaviour towards and treatment of others in the group
- How open-minded you are to another point of view
- Your listening skills
- Your ability to put forward your views and influence others
- Your leadership skills
- Your analytical skills and subject knowledge
- Your problem-solving skills
- Your attitude and confidence
- Whether you will fit into the culture of the company or not

There are a few types of GDs commonly conducted by companies. It is important for you to know in advance the type of GD that will be conducted by the companies visiting your campus so that you are able to prepare in advance for them.

a. **Topic-based GD:** In the topic-based GD, companies provide current and real topics for discussion, for example, 'Global warming and its effect on mankind',

'How are plastics affecting our earth?', 'Is the college degree creating more job seekers than job givers?', 'Indian economic growth since 1947'.

These fact-based GD topics require you to know the subject. Sometimes, you may be given a current controversial topic to assess your inclination, patience, anger control, creative thinking, and problem-solving and situation-handling capabilities. The topic could be 'The Farm Laws—advantages and disadvantages', or 'Arranged marriage or love marriage—which is better for society?'.

b. **Case- or article-based GD:** Here, you will be provided with a case study or article related to a business problem, sports, politics or technology, a few minutes before the start of the GD, and the group will be required to discuss a solution to the case. In the process, you will be assessed for your problem-solving and analytical skills and for your ability to think out of the box.

Approach and Tips for Group Discussion

For you, the objective in the group discussion is to get noticed positively so as to get shortlisted for the final interview. You must have a strategy to get noticed by the evaluators at the end of the session. Always have a paper and pen handy. The moment a topic is assigned, write down the key ideas, the sub-topics and the points that you would like to make on one side of a sheet of paper. Keep one half of the sheet for noting down the points raised by other members against their names. This will help you to address them individually or make a counter-point, mentioning them by name, when your turn comes. Making notes not only makes you look attentive, but also helps you structure your thoughts and understand and share different points of view even if you have limited knowledge of the topic.

When a topic is assigned and the group is asked to begin the discussion, try to take the lead. Introduce yourself and the other members of the group. Do not focus too much on yourself. If one of the group has taken the lead, then do not try to snatch the lead from that person or behave irresponsibly. Go with the flow, wait for your turn. If the discussion is going out of context, then try to take a lead in bringing it back on the rails. During the discussion, always appreciate others' point of view before adding your own.

For example, 'I appreciate Jeetendra's point of view'; add one or two sentences from what he said, and then say, 'I would like to add that (make your points)'. Just as initiating a group discussion helps to grab attention, similarly, summarization is an opportunity to turn heads and score points. Keep an eye on the watch, and just two minutes ahead of the scheduled end time, take the opportunity to summarize the discussion. Highlight the key points made by each member, and make a concluding remark. Do not forget to give due credit to all the participants for making the group discussion enriching and valuable.

There are a few essential points which are very important to get noticed and selected in a GD.

Appearance is the first thing to be noticed by anyone. Always wear formal attire and be well-groomed.

Maintain positive eye contact with the group in a consistent manner. This reflects your confidence. Avoid looking at the evaluator and concentrate on your peers. Listen actively and patiently, by slightly turning towards the candidate who is speaking, and use gestures, such as a nod in appreciation, in between.

Avoid dominance. Always remember, this is a group discussion and not a battle or debate. Be calm and have control of your voice, modulate it for pitch and decency. Respect others' views and do not try to dominate with your views or points. Being patient and calm is key.

Avoid interrupting others while they are talking. Wait for your turn. There could be a situation where you may want to cut short the speaker to make your point, then please do so politely with due respect and apologize for doing so.

For example: *'I am sorry to intervene, but considering the time limit, I may miss putting across my point, so I would like to say that . . . '*

Be confident and add good points. Choose your words wisely so as to make sure that each word spoken by you makes sense and creates an impact. **Avoid irrelevant talk and deviation from the topic.** Remember, **quality is more important than quantity.** Be short, simple and impactful.

Practice is key. Practise mock GDs with your friends to know your weak areas and improve on them.

5. **Technical Interview:** Companies do not expect you, as a fresher, to be a perfect fit for the role they are hiring for. But you must have certain technical skills to be considered fit for selection by the company. The technical interview is domain- and role-specific; it would vary based on the role the company is hiring for. During the technical interview, the focus will be the specific technical knowledge that the company requires in the candidate, his or her understanding of the technical competency required for the role in the company, practical application of such knowledge in real-life situations, clarity of thought, articulation and willingness to learn fast. You can expect interviewers to ask brain teasers, or to pose numerical reasoning or technical assessment problems that test your ability to create solutions and solve problems. The technical questions will vary, depending on your specialization and the role the company is hiring for.

How will you know what technical questions may come your way?

Review the job description given by the company. It will have the key skills and specific technical skills that the company is looking for. You also should research the company and find out what technical interview questions were asked by the company during its previous recruitment drives on campus. This will be immensely helpful and will give you a broad idea of what may be expected. Focus on basic applications, understanding of technical principles and methodologies. For example, if you specialize in automating testing software, review the processes for choosing test cases, application of the appropriate tools and creation of solutions that fix automated software issues. Practise solving technical problems and hone your own approach to solving problems. For example, you can use online portals to practise coding, building frameworks or building your data analysis skills. Besides asking technical questions, the interviewer would also be keen to know how you update your technical knowledge and learn new technical skills. So, in addition to technical questions, you can expect non-technical questions as well, such as:

- How do you keep your tech skills up-to-date?
- What are your favourite tech products to use, and why?
- Which are the three technologies or products that will be popular in the future, and why?
- How do you think technology can change the life of humans for the better?

You should do more than what everyone else does for staying ahead of them and getting selected. But, what exactly do you do to stay ahead of others?

'Do something others are not doing.'

One highly recommended way to differentiate yourself from others is to build your 'Skills Showcase Portfolio' and carry it with you. If you are a computer science or electronics student, then you should work on some software development project on your own and highlight that in your résumé. For example, you could develop a few simple projects, such as an Android or iOS app or a cool website. When you appear for your technical interview, carry your project with you and show it to the interviewer. If you are from a non-IT background, then work on a search model or create a mechanical model or design, or a robot or drone, or something like that related to your field. This will impress the interviewer, project you as being ahead of the others and reflect your proactiveness, in having gone beyond academics to learn to do something different.

6. **Panel and HR interview**: Interview techniques have been covered in detail in a separate chapter of this book, which you must understand to be successful in interviews. A panel interview, as the name suggests, is conducted by two or more interviewers. Most companies conduct panel interviews at campus to save time and to understand how candidates will operate in group situations. The panel interview will be similar to the normal interview. However, you should be prepared for fast-paced questions, cross-questioning and follow-up questions by the panel, and manage the different opinions and perspectives of the members.

   Again, preparation is the key for cracking this interview. You must research and find out more about the company whose panel interview you are going to attend. Here is an example of one company, Tata Consultancy Services:

Tata Consultancy Services (TCS) is an Indian multinational technology company that specializes in information technology, services and consulting. It is one of the largest IT companies in the world, with operations in 149 locations across forty-six countries. TCS recruitment happens throughout India, and all candidates are required to follow the same procedure. All the steps are mandatory for final selection. The complete process is known as 'TCS Ninja Hiring'.

The TCS interview process has three phases:

a)   Online registration
b)   Written/aptitude test
c)   Interview (technical and HR rounds)

a)   **Online Registration:** The process for any students starts with online registration
     • Register on TCS NextStep portal (TCS Careers) and create your profile.
     • Once the profile is created, log in with the registered email ID and password.
     • Fill the application form.
     • Complete your profile by uploading all the required documents.
     • After this, you will receive a venue for the aptitude test at a centre of your choice.

Eligibility: You must have a minimum aggregate of 60 per cent marks in all exams since Class X in the first attempt. A maximum of one pending backlog in the highest qualification is permitted at the time of applying, which should be cleared if you are selected. Only those candidates who have graduated from full-time courses, and with less than three years of work experience, are eligible.

b) **Written Test: TCS National Qualifier Test**

Once you successfully register and fill all the necessary details on the TCS NextStep portal, then you will receive the venue and date for the aptitude test, which is called the TCS National Qualifier Test. The TCS Ninja Test pattern and some solved previous-year papers are also available on the company portal. You can download the TCS Placement Question Papers and prepare for the test. The email writing section of the TCS Aptitude Written Test is also crucial. You must prepare for the tests going by the latest TCS placement papers.

The **TCS National Qualifier Test** consists of four rounds:
- Email writing test (one question, ten minutes).
- Quantitative ability and reasoning ability test (twenty questions, forty minutes).
- Programming language efficiency test (ten questions, twenty minutes).
- Coding test (one question, twenty minutes).

By email, you will be given instructions and a set of keywords. Follow the exact directions, and use all the keywords in the same order as listed in the question. Your answer should consist of a minimum of fifty words and a maximum of ninety words, if word length is not mentioned in the question.

Keep the sentence short, to the point, grammatically correct and without spelling mistakes.

In the analytical reasoning section, you will be tested for quantitative and reasoning ability within a limited time. Solve the easy questions first before attempting the difficult ones to save time and to maximize your score. Do not get obsessed with the 'star' questions that carry more marks. Move on if you do not know to solve them, and you can always come back to try them in the end if you have time.

The **programming language efficiency test** is a new round introduced by TCS, where you are expected to answer ten multiple-choice questions on C language, based on basic programming concepts.

The **coding test** is of the Command Line Programming type. You are required to solve one programming question in twenty minutes in C language, using an inbuilt online compiler.

c) **Interview:**

The **personal interviews** are done in three rounds, technical, managerial and HR.

The **technical interview** round will cover the general programming concepts. Knowledge of C language will be an added advantage. You must be prepared for detailed questions on the projects, summer internship or any other work mentioned by you in the résumé. You may also be asked to write programs.

The **managerial round** will be an interview aimed to assess how you will respond under pressure. You will be assessed from a holistic perspective for fitment into the respective account/project/business unit and the company. They will also check whether or not you can be trained in new areas. You may be given brain teasers, deliberately controversial questions, or you may meet with scepticism and emotional intimidation. In this round, you will be explained your career path, grade mapping and be given other relevant information about the company.

The **HR round** will assess you for your attitude and fitment into the role and culture of the company. You can expect the standard HR questions that we have shared in earlier chapters.

You must refer to the interview chapter of this book to prepare for these interviews.

Like the above example of TCS, the recruitment process of whichever company you are targeting for participation in their campus placement must be studied in detail. Companies keep changing their campus recruitment process every few years, which you must know about in advance. All information related to eligibility, the recruitment process and even support for preparation are available on individual company websites. You must use previous-year question papers and other available resources on the company's website to fully prepare for their hiring camp.

Campus placements are your best bet for getting a job, as you are competing against your peers. The recruitment process may seem rigorous, but a few weeks of serious and planned preparation makes the whole process easy and helps you get a job in your dream company.

Key Takeaways

1. Campus placements are your best bet for getting a job as you are in competition with your peers.
2. Know the company's campus recruitment process in advance.
3. Most of the information you need is available on the company website. Do customized preparation, as per the previous-year company recruitment patterns.
4. Build your 'Skill Showcase Portfolio'.

Exercise

1. Visit the websites of five companies that you are targeting for jobs and know their end-to-end campus hiring process.
2. Download test questions of the previous year, and practise solving them.
3. Practise group discussion with your friends, record your performance and work on areas that need improvement.

Useful Free Sites

1. **For Aptitude Tests:** You can practise mock aptitude tests free at www.practiceaptitudetests.com, www.testgorilla.com,

www.mock.sawaal.com and www.placement.freshersworld.com/
aptitude-questions-and-answers.

2. **Company-specific tests:** www.prep.youth4work.com/
   placement-papers has tests for many companies—
   Infosys, TCS, Capgemini, Deloitte, Accenture, Amazon,
   IBM, Tata Motors, Maruti, Reliance, L&T Infotech,
   Dell, HP, Oracle, Microsoft, Genpact, Ericsson, NTPC,
   Hero MotoCorp, Wipro, Paytm, Walmart, Yahoo and
   many more.

3. Technical Tests: You can do practical technical tests for
   each company at www.freshersworld.com, www.prep.
   youth4work.com/placement-papers, www.geeksforgeeks.org.

9

Things to Consider before Accepting a Job Offer

You have spent many weeks, maybe months, appearing for numerous interviews, waiting for a response and dealing with rejections. Finally, the day comes when you get an offer letter. You feel euphoric, invincible, important and literally on top of the world. If this is your first job and only offer in hand, then your choice is easy. Accept the offer.

But, if you are already working somewhere and making a decision to leave your current company and join the new one, then it is easy to get carried away. You will start feeling bad about everything in the current company—your role, the company culture, company policy and your boss. This feeling arises out of a bias, as you are more inclined to move on. The situation is quite similar to when you are dating someone. Everything looks just so perfect. If someone tells you that your reality is the opposite, you start feeling that the person is biased and not happy for you. But it is important to take a pause and evaluate the situation from a neutral perspective before you make a decision. Remember the old saying—the grass always looks greener on the other side! The recruiter at your prospective company will always lure you to sign on the dotted line in order to make you join the new company at the earliest. Calm your nerves, and think.

There are different types of offers. We have seen many examples in our careers, where a company has made a verbal offer to a candidate, and the candidate is in so much of a hurry that he has resigned from his current company. And, due to some reason, the new company does not give him a written offer, leaving him in deep trouble.

Here is a real-life example. One of India's top manufacturing companies (which we shall not name) was interviewing Partho (not his real name) for a senior position in the marketing department. He had three rounds of interview. For the final round, he was called to Pune to meet the managing director of the company. He travelled to Pune for the interview. The MD of the company interviewed him and liked him very much. Partho was asked to wait in the guest room. He was again called after thirty minutes into a big conference room. There were four people in the room—the MD, HR head, the president of a business vertical and the group HR head of the company. The MD asked him when he could join. Partho answered, 'I have three months' notice period at my current employer's and would be able to join within three months only.' The MD asked him a couple of general questions and finally extended his hand and said, 'Congratulations, you have been selected for this and we look forward to your joining at the earliest.' Partho exchanged customary pleasantries with everyone and returned. Within two days, he received a call from the human resources department of the company asking for his current compensation details. He shared them. Within the next two days, he received an email from the company with details of the compensation they were offering him. Partho was on top of the world. He thought of telling his current company about the offer and putting in his papers so that he could join the new company at the earliest. For some reason, he decided to wait for a few days. In the meantime, he sent his acceptance of the compensation offered him and requested to be sent the formal final offer letter. The final offer letter never reached him! Yes, you read it right. He did not receive a final offer letter from that big company! Imagine if he had broken the news to his current employer and had resigned!

You can debate whether this is right or ethical on that big company's part, but the fact of the matter is, these things happen. One step in a hurry can jeopardize your career, at least for some time. You need to have patience.

There are many types of job offers that can be made by a company:

- *Verbal offer*: Like you, the company is also excited to find the right candidate for itself. Some hiring manager from HR can get very excited and make you a verbal offer immediately after your interview or within days of it. This person may be keen to know how serious you are about the job and how soon you can join. You can ask for more information on what you want to know at this stage. Be happy that the company is making you the offer, but do not make any decision based on a verbal offer. Show enthusiasm, thank the person who made the offer, and then ask when you can expect a written contract or offer.

- *Sharing of compensation details by email*: After making a verbal offer, most companies send you a compensation sheet for you to accept. This will have the details related to the role, location, compensation and benefits offered you by the company. Take your time to compare them with your current compensation and benefits. If you are satisfied, please confirm this and request for a written formal offer/contract.

- *Written offer*: A written job offer is a comprehensive two-to-four-page offer letter on the letterhead of the company. This will be signed by the company and will have a place for you to sign and accept the offer. Review the document for compensation, role, terms, conditions and date of joining before signing it and sending it back to the company. If you are currently in a job, please make sure that the date of joining mentioned in the offer letter allows you sufficient time to serve your notice period or be relieved from your current job.

It is important to accept the job offer only after understanding every aspect of it. This will help you avoid nasty surprises later and will leave you with no reason to complain after you have joined the company. It is good for you as well as for the company that a satisfied employee with no baggage is joining.

Everyone has their own priorities when it comes to building a successful career. However, when it comes to reality, things can get quite tricky. One needs to evaluate a job offer based on many different aspects—salary, benefits, work culture, company brand, role, your immediate boss and the team which you are going to join. This essentially means that everyone would have their own set of drivers when it comes to accepting a job offer. However, while certain things are personal, there are six things that everyone must evaluate and analyse very carefully and be thoroughly satisfied about before accepting a job offer.

1. Company, role and designation (CRD)

CRD is what we recommend as the first aspect to be considered. We are recommending this based on our personal experience and the experience of many others who have shared their career journeys after working for decades in the corporate world.

In 2010–11, Subir was general manager and hub HR head at Reliance Communications Limited, and was heading HR for more than 2,000 employees. He had a very good track record of consistent high performance and promotion in the company. In fact, Subir was the youngest hub HR head in the country. He was familiar with people and a favourite of his boss on account of his exceptional work. One day, he got a call from a consultant for the role of chief human resource officer in a United Kingdom-based telecom company, which was starting operations in India. It was a relatively small company. However, since the role (CHRO) and the compensation were very good, he thought this was a godsend for him to take his career to the next level! He decided to join the company. For the first three months, life was high-flying and rocking. Subir's salary was more than double his salary at Reliance. The company provided him fully furnished accommodation at Delhi, business class travel, reimbursement for weekend parties, an informal work environment, global experience and a lot more. Subir could not have asked for more. In fact, around the same time, the company hired a few senior leadership team members too, all from good companies like Ericsson, Airtel, etc. Their reason for joining too must have been similar to Subir's. Four months passed . . . One day, Subir and the other new joiners came to know that due to some development at the promoters' end and external market conditions, the company's launch had been delayed. Everything started to look uncertain. Panic started building among the employees as the company did not now appear to have a solid financial foundation to sustain for even a few months!

Subir realized that he made a mistake by joining this company!

With so many venture capital-funded start-ups having come up, and given the earlier growth in the economy, the situation remains similar to the one Subir faced, now that tough times have come. Hence, we believe and advise everyone else to give the company's brand, name and culture top priority when considering a job opportunity or job change.

We have seen many people joining companies only for the designation and salary they have been offered. In our view, this may not be the right decision if you are from a middle-class family and do not have a degree from a premier college. People from a financially sound background or those who have qualifications from premier colleges can take chances, as even if they fail they have the support of a strong brand or have money to fall back on. If you are looking for a long-term career, the company brand is equally, if not more, important than designation and salary. In the current turbulent market environment and tough economic conditions, a company with an established brand and credibility will ensure that it will sail through short- and mid-term turbulence without any impact on its employees.

After the durability of the company brand, the next priority for you to consider should be your role in the company. That is what determines the quality of work and experience you will have at the company. While the role can keep evolving, at the initial stage it should have clearly defined responsibilities and expectations, to avoid your having to face any performance and expectation gaps after you join the company. It is recommended that you connect with more people in the company to gather more information and also to validate what you have been officially promised.

Designation will define your position in the organizational hierarchy of the company while also clarifying what responsibilities and authority have been assigned to you as part of the job. Some companies, like the traditional manufacturing and IT sectors, have a limited variety of roles to offer. Some are liberal and offer many (sometimes too many) designations, as in the finance, retail and services sectors. You should not compare across sectors, but within sectors when you evaluate your designation.

2. Your relationship with your manager is like a marriage; know the person well before committing

In most cases, you will get to meet your future manager during the interview process. This is the most important aspect that you must keep in mind, as you are going to be stuck for a significant amount of time with this person. She/he will be directly responsible for your learning, growth, performance and engagement in the organization, as well as your career.

Therefore, it is very important to have a manager that you can look up to, who is personally interested in not only achieving the organizational goals and his own personal development but is also equally invested in the growth and progress of his team members. It is advisable to inquire from the recruiter or HR about your reporting manager and ensure that you collect information from a few current and previous employees who have worked with him, in addition to exploring other sources, like social media, before accepting the job offer.

It is hard to change someone's attitude. If you have received negative feedback about a manager from multiple sources, then think again before joining his team. If you are already in a job and doing well, then we would advise you not to join that company if you have to work with such a person. But, if you are a fresher or currently not in a job, then you do not have a choice.

3. Salary and benefits

The term cost to company (CTC) is more often than not illusory and difficult to understand for many, as each company's CTC consists of different components. While job aspirants are often interested in the final amount being offered them, companies often have a complex pay structure, under which your salary may be divided under different heads, such as basic, flexi-pay, duty allowance, special allowance, conveyance, fuel, pension, provident fund and others. Some of these heads are part of your CTC but will not make it to your in-hand salary, which you receive every month. Understand well what your gross, net cash-in-hand monthly and annual salaries will be.

Another aspect that you must look for as far as salary is concerned, is the salary potential of a particular role and the market standing of the compensation being offered for similar roles in the same industry. Simply put, it means that your salary and your designation should complement each other. For instance, if you are an executive and are being offered an annual CTC package of Rs 4 lakh per annum, against the current market standing of Rs 8 lakh per annum for the same number of years of experience in the same industry, then you should reconsider (if you have a job in hand) your offer, as whenever you switch jobs, your new compensation package would be determined on the basis of your current compensation.

4. Cash and non-cash benefits

Benefits, both cash and non-cash, are important and vary from company to company. You should give due importance to this element too. In addition to the salary components, many job offers come with their own sets of cash and non-cash benefits, such as the percentage of medical insurance premium paid by the company for employee and family, including dependent parents/in-laws, company-owned accommodation, company-leased accommodation, company car, dental and OPD medical reimbursement, mobile handset, monthly mobile and data bill reimbursement, etc. In addition to compensation, you must consider these benefits, especially housing and medical, to compare in totality the proposed offer with your current compensation.

5. Find out about the company's past increment and bonus payout trends

Many sectors have different policies and follow different trends when it comes to annual increments and payment of bonus to their employees, and companies within these sectors follow their own trends too. The annual increment varies from 2 per cent to 20 per cent, depending on some factors, like individual, department and company performance. Some companies calculate increment as a percentage of only the fixed component of the salary, whereas some calculate increments as a variable of the CTC. Some companies may pay bonus of up to 150 per cent of the annual performance pay component of your salary. By knowing these payment trends of the company, you can compare the increments and performance pay amounts offered to you with that at your current company. These two factors would have a substantial and reoccurring financial impact if you are looking to work for more than three years in the company.

6. Learning opportunities and career development

You must ask questions about the company's career development opportunities and understand what learning and development opportunities are provided by the company through in-house training, higher education opportunities, professional development opportunities and related policies. In today's world, continuous learning is the most important aspect to remain relevant and ensure your career progression. A progressive company offers many learning opportunities, and this is essential for your future career growth.

When you are satisfied with having assessed your offer for all these aspects, sign the offer letter and send it back to the recruiter. If you have negotiated or asked for any changes, make sure you get a new offer letter that has all the changes. Generally, you will receive an offer letter as an email attachment. Take a printout of the attachment, sign it, scan it and send it back as an attachment as an acceptance of the offer. Keep the original offer letter safely.

You are building a new relationship which is very important for you. Use this opportunity to thank the company and express your interest in the role that has been offered, creating a positive impression of yourself again. The acceptance email should be well written. The subject line of the email should clearly convey the purpose of the email. A simple subject line can be 'Acceptance of offer letter from [Your Name]'. In the email, thank the hiring manager and/ or the recruiter for giving you the chance to work with the company, express gratitude and enthusiasm for the role and how excited you are to work with them. Volunteer to help and contribute even before joining. You can write that you will be happy to contribute even before joining them and that it will be your pleasure to be part of any assignment even before your formal joining.

You can use the following format for your email:

Subject line: Offer Acceptance - [Your Name]

Dear Mr/Ms [name of the recruiter or person who sent you the offer or email],

I am extremely pleased to formally accept the offered position as [role offered to you] with [name of the company] and am looking forward to contributing to the success of the company.

As you are aware, I have been working in [name of your current company if you are working] for the last two years. I will start the separation process here and will be handing over my current responsibilities at the earliest. Though my notice period is three months, I will request for early relief here and will confirm my exact joining date in a few days.

It will be my pleasure to be involved in any assignment to which you think I can add value to even before joining.

You can reach me at [phone number] and [email address].

Looking forward to meeting you and joining the company soon.

Yours sincerely,
[Your Name]

Joining a company is a big decision and must be taken after considering all aspects and keeping in mind the long term. Do not take this decision in a hurry or base it on any emotional reasons. No company or team is perfect. If you are already employed, decide to jump ship only if you are fully convinced that this move will take you further ahead along the right path of career growth.

Key Takeaways

1. You must find out the following in detail before accepting an offer to join a new company:
   a. CRD—Company, your role and responsibility and designation
   b. Your future manager and his/her working style
2. Understand the salary components and the benefits provided by the company.
3. Find out what your non-cash and cash benefits will be.
4. Find out the past trends related to increment and bonus payouts at the new company.
5. Find out the HR policies of the company related to performance appraisal and promotion.

Exercise

Take your previous CTC offer, or anyone's salary if you haven't worked anywhere, and calculate your net in-hand salary, gross salary and annual CTC.

Useful Free Sites

1. **Glassdoor:** This portal carries reviews of the culture, salary, interviews, business outlook and the leadership team at various companies by their current and previous employees. It has descriptions of real experiences and feedback from these employees on the good and bad about the companies and their processes. You must read these reviews to assess the company that has offered you a job. The portal also provides useful information about the compensation range offered for various roles and the benefits offered by companies. This will help you in your decision-making.

2. **Quora**: This is basically a question-and-answer site. You can ask questions that you would like answered. People will respond sharing their knowledge, perspectives, opinions and ideas. It is a great way to gain an outside perspective on working for a particular company. If you do not want to post your question yourself, then you can search for questions and answers posted by others to get the desired insights.

3. **CareerBliss**: This portal too, like Glassdoor, provides insights into companies. You can find out more about a particular company—its culture, the people you are going to work with, growth opportunities and work environment.

10

Be Unique; Get an Edge with a Video Résumé

Video résumés are serious game changers!

Videos allow you to share your journey in the form of storytelling, which is an engaging, unique, innovative and imaginative way to profile yourself. In the new digital world, most people are moving from 'read' to 'watch' mode. People prefer to watch videos rather than read text-based content due the highly visual nature and recall value of the former, making it easier for them to remember and absorb the content. According to a survey, 73 per cent of people have less time to read and do not want to read, and 51 per cent prefer to watch video.* On a professional networking platform like LinkedIn,

---

* There are a few surveys done by video marketing firms, which can be accessed at https://www.convinceandconvert. com/content-marketing/video-marketing-statistics/ (Kayla Matthews, '12 Video Marketing Statistics You Need to Know in 2020', convinceandconvert.com) and

members spend nearly 3x more time watching video than reading. Like everyone else, recruiters too are often pressed for time in today's fast-moving world.

Everyone has a traditional text résumé. Your résumé needs to get the right attention for you to be called for a job interview. Most résumés get rejected at this stage itself. The competition in the job market is fierce. You need to find ways to grab the eyeballs of the recruiter. One of the ways to do so is through a **video résumé.** It gives an opportunity to the recruiter to judge you by the way you speak, your facial expressions, your body language and your creativity. In the process, you may also score some unexpected brownie points. If you are an active job seeker, then your video posted on social media can easily be shared by others, thus helping you reach a large number of recruiters in the minimum possible time. A video résumé is an incredible way to show off your personality, experience, qualifications and soft skills by using technology in the shortest possible time. You are more likely to be hired because of your video résumé than other candidates who have only a traditional résumé to show, everything else being equal. A video résumé is preferred by recruiters also, as it is a much faster way of getting an idea of who you are and helps them save time.

A video résumé (commonly known as visumé or video CV) is a new way to present your abilities. You can also use this to force-apply, by sharing your short video résumé with some recruiters and people in your networks.

---

https://www.retaildive.com/news/72-of-consumers-prefer-videos-to-text-marketing/524161/ (Dan Alaimo, '72 Per Cent of Consumers Prefer Videos to Text Marketing', *Retail Dive*, 23 May 2018).

Most companies are adapting to the virtual way of working. Employees' physical presence at work is reducing day by day. Interviewing candidates over the virtual medium is a low-cost hiring method for employers. As employers are becoming more comfortable with video technologies, job seekers should use them to impress prospective employers even before any actual interview. One of the best ways to do this is by making a video résumé, and we recommend early adoption of technology by you to make one for yourself.

A video résumé is a 60- to 120-second-long video in which you, as a job seeker, can highlight your qualifications, skills, accomplishments, experience, soft skills and other relevant key points about yourself, which will encourage companies to call you for an interview.

Today, the competition for jobs being fierce, it is very difficult for your résumé to get noticed during the screening process from among thousands of applications that any company receives. Just crafting a professional three-page résumé will not make you stand out from the crowd.

You have to use multiple channels to reach out and get noticed by companies so that you get an interview call.

Many recruiters today prefer these résumés to the traditional paper résumé, as they are able to see and hear you. Their task of initial shortlisting becomes easier. Many job sites are adopting this trend and have incorporated changes to accept video résumés.

While video résumés can be used by every job seeker, it is particularly recommended for direct customer-facing job profiles in industries like hotel and hospitality, retail, call centres, media, public relations, event management and other customer-facing roles. A video résumé is a better way to showcase your charming personality and your communication and presentation skills. This can be the easiest way for you to get an interview call from a company.

A video résumé should be unique, creative and professionally made. It is easy to make and can also be created at home. You can also hire a professional to make it. If you are making a video résumé for the first time, then the most important thing is to prepare and practise for it. Here are some tips:

1. Write a short, simple and straightforward script

Your script should be like an interesting story that anyone would like to hear. Write down your educational details, key achievements, work experience, projects and competencies that are relevant for the job in question. Keep your focus on the requirements of the job and pay more attention to the company requirements than yourself, and talk about why the company should hire you. Use simple and easy-to-understand language without any jargon. Your video must end with why you want to join the company and why the company should select you.

You can refer to the sample script below to write your personal script.

Ideally, the duration of your video résumé should be one minute, but it can go up to two minutes.

2. Look natural and do not read the résumé while recording

Memorize the script, look natural, and record. If you are targeting multiple roles, then record more videos, mentioning the skills and experience relevant to the different positions you are considering. Do not be afraid to talk about your passions. Be creative and different, within professional boundaries.

3. Watch out for light, background, voice speed and volume

Your background, and the light in the room, should be good so that the video is clear and looks professional. Speak slowly and clearly, and be audible. Speak just as you do in formal conversations. Look into the camera of the phone, and avoid excessive hand and eye movement. This will produce the impression that you are quite confident. The best camera angle for this would cover your face and chest while you are sitting in a chair. This position will also make you look calmer.

4. Look presentable and wear formal attire

You must be presentable and well groomed. Do not wear loud clothes for the video. Muted blue is a nice colour and always makes you look good.

5. How to edit your final video résumé

If your video does not meet your expectation, then editing is an option. You can check the quality of your video as well as the content. If your recorded video has some fillers like 'ok', 'right', 'ummm . . . ', 'ahhh . . . ', 'like', you can edit them out and properly adjust the volume.

6. Get feedback from your friends

Share your final video résumé with a few of your friends and seniors and ask for their feedback. You might have overlooked some silly errors while making the video. Getting feedback from other people is a very important step. You can make edits and changes based on their suggestions.

Your script should run like this:
1. You introduce yourself.
2. Thank your viewers for watching.
3. Talk about your education (where you went to school, college name and place), work experience (companies you worked with), achievements, and finally, your personal attributes and your passions.
4. Dwell on your job experiences, projects and volunteering, and describe your skills (which the job you are targeting requires). You can also share your favourite professional experiences and professional successes. Then, talk about what you can bring to the new company and express interest in the job and company.

5. In the end, you must thank your viewers and share your contact information.

A sample script outline for an electrical engineer with some experience:

Hi, my name is Sumit. I will be sharing with you some information about the exciting and certainly never boring world of the energy sector in sixty seconds. Do watch till the end.

While completing my BTech in electrical engineering from Patna University, I never thought about coal or natural gas, wind or solar energy. All of *my energy* was concentrated on being a standout student, which I achieved, ranking among the top ten in the university.

I spent the next two years working in operation and maintenance at the NALCO plant at Angul in Odisha. Besides winning the best employee award, I also developed my social skills, communications skills, and my ability to manage community members and vendors.

My career took off quickly after that, and I eventually made my way to the position of assistant manager at Hindalco, Rourkela. Little did I know that the local, regional and political contacts that I made would serve me well when I found myself working for a Fortune 500 energy company. After only a year and a half, I was promoted as manager, maintenance, and my responsibilities further increased! My people skills were really put to the test during this time, when I spent many days dealing with unions, external stakeholders and angry villagers who were facing mining or drilling on their property. I discovered that, often, a kind word and a willing ear are important to reassure the angry property owner. I learned that a company is only as good as the people it sends out into the community.

Can I be that person for you? I know the energy industry, from coal mining to natural gas drilling to solar to wind.

I'm looking forward to taking our relationship to the next level and meeting you in person. I can be reached at 9999999999. Thank you for taking the time to watch my video. I look forward to hearing from you.

Write your script, record, edit, and start sharing your video résumé. Besides being unique, it will be impactful and will bring better results in your job search.

Some of you who are doing it for the first time may be camera-shy and may feel uncomfortable. Do not worry. Understand that it will take a few repetitions before you are able to make the perfect video. Record, watch and correct. Re-record if you are not satisfied with the results. Keep the above tips in mind and you will soon record your ultimate video résumé.

If you are not comfortable facing the camera, you can use animation, the whiteboard and the stop motion mode of video résumé. But we strongly recommend that you face the camera and record a video résumé to create a better impact.

How to Share Your Video Résumé

Congratulations. Your video résumé is ready.

You can upload your video on your personal social media pages or on YouTube. Include your video résumé link in your text résumé. With this you are providing recruiters, who will receive your traditional résumé, with access to your video résumé.

Add the video résumé link in your email signature. With this you are sharing your video résumé with the recruiters you want to target.

Avoid sharing your video on WhatsApp, Telegram or Google Chat messages. Rather, share the link with a brief message.

While sharing your CV on social media or sending forced applications on social media or by email, always include the link of the video. This will provide recruiters/connections the option to watch it and also share it with their connections if they want to refer you to someone.

Finally, do not expect your video résumé to replace your traditional résumé. New-age companies may prefer a video résumé; however, some of the traditional companies may still prefer a traditional résumé. The video résumé is an excellent tool for job search. You should use it selectively and where you feel it will create an impact.

Key Takeaways

1. Write a short, simple and crisp script before making your video résumé.
2. Put on a formal attire and look well groomed.
3. Make sure you have proper lighting on the face and a clear background.

4. Be calm, pleasant, speak clearly and slowly.
5. Edit your video to remove any unwanted portions.
6. Share with a few friends and relatives for feedback.
7. Work on feedback to fine-tune your résumé before finalizing it.

Exercise

Write the script for your video résumé.

Useful Free Sites/Tools

1. **https://biteable.com/corporate/resume/:** This site helps you create free video résumés in a few minutes. It has ready-to-use templates too.
2. **https://www.renderforest.com/video-resume:** This site offers you templates based on your targeted roles, like content writer, graphic designer, event manager, etc. You can choose your targeted role and create your video résumé.
3. **CareerBuilder.com and Vault.com** also accept video résumés and provide helpful tips for creating one.
4. **Your mobile phone:** You can shoot your video résumé with your mobile phone and edit it using the various mobile apps available.
5. **Editing tools:** Some of the free video editing tools are InShot, OpenShot, Movie Maker and Canva. There are many options available, depending on the software you are using.

11

Virtual Interviews Are the Future

Easier Internet access and developments in technology have vastly changed the way job interviews are conducted. Companies are focusing increasingly on virtual interaction for many of their activities, including job interviews and the shortlisting of candidates for face-to-face interviews. Virtual interaction is an ideal way to interview candidates scattered in different locations over a large geography, as neither the candidate nor the interviewer needs to travel for the interview. For companies, it has reduced the hiring cycle time and has improved the quality of hires as they are able to target candidates from all locations. Virtual interviews are also convenient because they can accommodate a variety of schedules. For example, if you are in a full-time job, you may not be able to travel for an in-person interview during normal working hours. Virtual interviews allow you to appear for such interviews. Often, we find that good candidates are reluctant to visit an office for face-to-face interviews for reasons of confidentiality. Virtual interviews help companies interview such candidates; this ensures that they do not lose out on candidates with excellent qualifications and experience simply because of logistical reasons. During the recent COVID-19 pandemic, the virtual interview has reached its peak usage and has ensured that recruitment takes place as usual.

Virtual interviews benefit both companies and candidates in many ways, making this method of interview very popular.

- **Access to the best talent:** People of high quality, and those with niche skills or domain expertise, are always in demand. It may be difficult for them to attend a physical interview. The virtual mode provides flexibility to both companies and such job aspirants.
- **Time and cost saving:** The virtual interview saves a lot of time as it does away with the need for a candidate to travel to the interview, and this means cost savings for both too. Naturally, hiring time is also reduced. Both company and candidate also get to know the outcome of the interview faster.
- **Access to talent from across the globe:** The virtual interview allows companies to interview talents from anywhere in the world without the recruiters having to move out of their offices.

Virtual communication requires special considerations and preparation because of possible technical problems and time-zone issues. As a candidate using a laptop, desktop or phone for your virtual interview, you may face connectivity issues due to technical faults in the hardware, software or the network you use. All this is not in your control, but would leave a negative impression if it happens during the interview.

As the name suggests, a virtual interview is a digital way for recruiters to remotely interact with candidates, either through the medium of video or audio. It takes place remotely, over the phone or through videoconferencing and other online communication platforms. There are mainly three types of virtual interview:

1. Live video interview
2. Recorded interview/interview by robots
3. Phone interview

Virtual interviews are often conducted much the same way as face-to-face interviews. There are many guides available on how best to do face-to-face interviews. Here, we will focus on the virtual interview, whose importance is increasing with every passing day. Mastering this form of interview is critical for success in your job search.

Like the face-to-face interview, the virtual interview can also be one-to-one or one-to-many. For the virtual interview, it is important to take care of a few critical aspects to ensure your success.

1. Live video interview

a. **Before a virtual interview:**
i. **Schedule and block your calendar by sending an invite on email, or accept meeting request:** If your interview date and time are scheduled, wait to receive a calendar invite from the company; it will have the

date and time of the interview, the duration, and other
details. Accept the invite to confirm your attendance.
In case you do not get an invite, please get in touch
with the recruiter so that an invitation is sent to you.
A calendar meeting invite gives everyone an early
intimation to join the interview before the scheduled
time. We have seen many interviews getting delayed
or not taking place at all as scheduled because the
interviewer did not have his or her calendar blocked.
In the absence of a proper invite, the meeting was not
visible on his or her calendar, and the slot was allocated
for some other purpose. Most virtual meetings will
need an access code or a password to log in. Make
sure you have these details. You should also know the
duration of the interview, and whether any documents,
or other information, are required for it.

The larger benefit of the meeting invite is to
find out more about the interviewer. A meeting
invite for the interview will have the email ID of
the interviewer, as most recruiters send invites to
interviewers to block their calendar. The email ID
in the meeting invite gives you an opportunity to
search for more information about the interviewer
so that you can be better prepared for the interview.

ii. **Arrange your set-up well—the location, lighting,
camera and equipment**
You are like a star. You need to make sure that the
room you are sitting in is clean, with proper lighting
on your face and a clean wall behind your back to
ensure minimum distraction at the interview. Ensure

that you are the focal point of the conversation. Avoid using your bedroom or couch, and preferably place your computer on a table instead of on your lap or elsewhere, where any shaking can create disturbance during the interview.

The angle and focus of the camera are very important factors. Avoid placing the camera too close or too far. Place it in such a manner that your portrait (top half of your body) is visible on the screen. This will allow interviewers to see your hand gestures and make it easier for them to gauge your overall body language. The light in the room should be bright. The light should be focused (whether it is natural or artificial light) on your face, which must be properly visible. No part of your face should be in shadow.

It will be good if you can turn off the TV, close all the windows of the room and keep the cell phone in silent mode.

iii. **Use a secure Internet connection and become familiar with videoconferencing tools**
The last thing you would want is the Internet getting disconnected in the middle of your virtual interview. It is recommended that you use wired Internet or reliable data connectivity for better stability. You should close all the applications in your system, like high-definition video or online games. Double-check your camera and the sound settings in your computer. You should use earphones with good sound clarity.

Software such as Skype, Zoom, Webex, Google Hangouts, JioMeet and WhatsApp are available; they can be a bit overwhelming if you have not used them before. Make yourself familiar with the features—mute, screen sharing, video off–on, notes, chat, and other facilities of the video-conferencing platform—well before the interview. You should also know how to fix minor problems if anything inexplicably stops working during the interview. Being naïve or appearing not very techno-savvy will give the impression that you are not good at basic technology, and the interviewer will doubt if you are the right candidate for the position.

We highly recommend that you log in ten to fifteen minutes before your interview. Check your Internet connection and turn on the sound and video to ensure that everything is in order. Once you are sure that everything is working fine, you can mute the app and wait for the interviewer to join in. After the interview, do not be in a hurry to leave the meeting. This may be viewed as rude. Allow the interviewer to leave the meeting first.

iv. **Prepare, practise and give a virtual interview as if it were a face-to-face interview**
You may feel uncomfortable initially, if you are not already familiar with the virtual interview. For example, a face-to-face interview would normally start and end with a formal handshake. This is not possible in a virtual interview. So, you should practise

greeting your interviewer professionally, keeping in mind that you will be appearing in a virtual interview. For example, you should slightly nod your head or subtly raise your hand while greeting your interviewer. Most candidates look into their screen during a virtual interaction; they are under the impression that they are looking at the interviewer. Instead, practise looking at the camera while talking instead of looking directly at the on-screen image of the interviewer. **Virtual eye contact** is an important skill to master, to create an impactful first impression. Just as you would in an in-person interview, you should answer in-depth all the questions you are asked. You must practise your answers to potential interview questions to feel comfortable and confident at the actual interview. Always keep a printout of your résumé at hand.

v. **Keep 'key achievements' file/presentation ready**
    You must use the virtual interview tools to your advantage. Prepare a presentation of all your achievements and work you want to showcase. Use the opportunity at the end of the interview to use the share feature of videoconferencing. If you get permission, show/talk about your achievements. This will leave a good impression on the interviewer. It will also reflect positively on you and let the interviewer know how serious you are about the job in the company.

vi. **Dress appropriately**

Be professionally dressed, even if it is a virtual interview. You will feel more comfortable, confident and competent in formal business attire. It will also convey your seriousness to the interviewer. Do not wear professional attire on top and casual shorts below. You never know, you may need to get up during the interview, maybe to pick up a pen you dropped, or to address any other issue that may arise during the interview.

b. **During the interview:**

i. **Watch your body language:**

Look into the camera and converse. Do not look at yourself in the bottom right-hand corner of the screen where your small video is visible. The interviewer is likely to pick your erratic eye movement and may conclude that you are someone who loves himself. In fact, the interviewer may even think that you are taking some external help during the interview. Make eye contact with the interviewer by looking at him through the web cam, as you would in a face-to-face interview. Deliberately create a feeling of relaxation within, as that will make your body language look better. Sit straight while facing the web cam and do not slouch or lean back or cross your arms. Be alert and look ready to answer questions. The main way to communicate confidence is to sit up straight, smile and keep the camera at eye level.

ii. **Speak with clarity, your voice at the right pitch and at average speed:**
Unlike a face-to-face conversation, the virtual interview generally has a lag of a few micro-seconds. Ensure that you enunciate your words clearly, speaking in a moderately loud voice and at moderate speed. During the interview, listen carefully and wait for a question to be finished before you start to answer.

iii. **Be your natural self and build rapport immediately:**
In a video interview, you should focus more on your verbal communication. If you are excited about the role, you should sound excited. Tell the interviewers with enthusiasm that you are pleased to meet them, because many of your non-verbal cues, such as facial expressions and hand gestures, may be lost due to low video-quality or because your body is not fully visible in the frame. It is not easy to connect with everyone, but speaking with enthusiasm is a crucial requirement in a virtual interview. You want the interviewer to be able to remember a personal story you told or a common interest you shared.

iv. **Maintain your focus:**
We have seen many candidates doodling on paper, browsing on another tab, answering emails, attending to notifications or sending messages during their virtual interview. It is common and very easy to get

distracted during a virtual interview, unlike during an in-person interview. This shows your casual attitude towards the interviewer. The interviewer is monitoring you. Due to your eye movements and body language, your distraction will be easily noticed by the interviewer. Avoid the temptation to browse or to check your emails and **turn off all notifications** to avoid any distraction. Stay fully focused and be present with your body and mind for the interview.

c. **After the interview:**

i. **Send an impactful thank-you email or message within thirty minutes of the interview:**
A virtual interview gives you access to the email ID of the interviewer and the HR personnel. Use it to your advantage. Just after finishing the interview, write a good thank-you letter highlighting something the interviewer said, showing your interest in the role, in the company, and in working with the interviewer. Since the company may be interviewing many others, it will be best to send a thank-you email or message within thirty minutes of your interview.

After a couple of days, send some articles or research papers relevant to the industry, company or your role to the interviewer and recruiter. This will impress the interviewer and would also work as a reminder to him or her that you were interviewed. Repeat this once a week. Even if you are not selected for the job, keep in touch with the interviewer and build a relationship with him or her. This will force the interviewer to consider you for future vacancies or refer you to his or her friends in the industry.

ii. Review your performance:

If you are new to the virtual interview, spend a few minutes to look back and write what went well and what you could have done better at your interview. Remember your childhood days, when after an examination you would calculate your probable marks against each question after referring to your friends' answers or checking the answers from the textbook? This is a good practice for any interview format too, especially for a virtual interview, where there are additional factors to consider.

2. Recorded or robotic interview

Recorded or robotic interviews are a little different from live virtual interviews, as you will be interviewed not by a human but by a robot or by means of pre-recorded questions. An artificial intelligence robot has stepped into the recruiting space for interviewing. Use of AI-based robots is likely to increase in a big way in the future, as they remove human limitations such as working hours. These robots can work 24*7 and conduct interviews at any time. Also, when programmed correctly, AI can weed out some of the implicit biases that recruiters have. These robots are equipped with AI, sentiment analysis, facial recognition, video analytics, neural language processing, machine learning and speech recognition. These robots also use deep learning to deliver a human-like conversation to the candidate. They understand context, complex multipart statements and changed answers.

You may have already appeared in a few robotic interviews. If not, you will come across them very soon.

You will be asked a series of questions and be required to record your answers and submit them. With this format, you will likely be given around two minutes of recording time for each question. It's important that you are familiar with all aspects of the role and business you are applying for. In this type of interview, in addition to the points mentioned for the live virtual interview, you need to be crisp and to the point so that your answers cover all aspects of the questions in the limited period of time given to you. Performance is assessed based on your facial expressions, gestures, sentiment analysis of your voice, your knowledge, competencies, cultural fitment and personality. The software matches your response with the attributes required for the job, which are already programmed into the system.

You should take the interview by robots as seriously as you would any other virtual interview. Adhere to all the guidelines, as these robots are quick and consistent in observing your answers and attributes and in providing detailed insights about you to the company.

3. Telephonic interview

In practice, the telephonic interview even today is the most widely used and convenient mode of interview for the initial screening of candidates for shortlisting for face-to-face in-person or virtual interviews. This is the most cost-effective and efficient method to screen available, suitable and affordable candidates. Again, you should take it as seriously as you would take a traditional face-to-face meeting. Besides interview techniques, there are some exclusive telephonic interview guidelines you should keep in mind.

Again, preparation and practice are key.

Before the interview, use a voice recorder to practise and to know how others hear you on the phone. Practising a mock interview over the phone with your mentor or senior would be useful. You should keep your CV in front of you. Also keep a 'cheat paper' in front of you. This cheat paper should have the key points and achievements that you want to highlight. Do not write entire paragraphs, but just the key bullet points. You can refer to this paper and put across the best points at the relevant time during your telephonic interview. Turn off call waiting so you are not interrupted. You should schedule your virtual interview call before or after office hours so that you are not in a hurry to reach office and do not have to take the call while travelling.

During the interview, make sure that you have good earphones for better two-way voice clarity. Speak slowly, clearly and directly into the phone receiver. Your voice modulation should be good and the tone of your voice should convey that you are normal, confident and, above all, interested in talking to the person at the other end. Avoid the use of 'filler' words or sounds like 'ah', 'hum', 'uhhh' and 'okay'. In place of a simple yes or no response, answer using full sentences, mentioning your selling points at every opportunity by backing up your answers with descriptions of your work, qualifications and experience in that context. Avoid single-word answers. Write notes, making points from the questions and your own answers. It is good to ask how the interviewer would like to be addressed. Do not straightaway start with the first name as you may not be aware about the seniority of the caller. If you are not sure or do not want to ask, it is safer to address the interviewer as Sir or Madam. Never hang up the phone first. Let the caller hang up first. Be pleasant and speak with a warm smile. A smile can be 'heard' over the telephone.

After the interview, review your notes to go through what you were asked. Evaluate your performance and practise to improve your future telephonic interviews. Always follow up the interview with a thank-you email as it re-emphasizes your interest in the job. Do not forget to mention the discussion points in brief in your note, as advised earlier.

The key to success in all types of virtual interviews is familiarity with the tools and proper preparation and practice. From ensuring your technology is working to conducting your research before the meeting, to being poised (sitting down at your computer or using your phone) and ready for any question that may come your way will help set you apart from other applicants. These types of interviews are the future. If you want to stay ahead of others, practise and master them.

You must ensure that your personality shines through, whether it is an in-person interview or a digital one.

Key Takeaways

1. The virtual interview is the new norm and is important to master for success in a job interview.
2. Familiarize yourself with the various features of virtual tools before the interview.
3. Set right the lighting, background, sound, etc., so that you are clearly visible and remain the focal point during the interview.
4. Prepare a presentation of your achievements, which you can share during the interview.
5. Send a thank-you note within thirty minutes of the interview.
6. Connect weekly with the interviewer to remain fresh in the mind of the company.

Exercise

1. Practise a dummy interview session with your relatives or friends on a virtual medium.
2. Record your interview, watch and improve on it.
3. Use virtual tools (Zoom, JioMeet, Skype, Google Hangouts, Webex, Microsoft Teams) to familiarize yourself with their features.

Useful Free Sites

1. **Virtual video calling portal:** Create free account with Zoom, JioMeet, Google Hangouts, etc., and make yourself familiar with their features. Practise with each

tool by connecting with friends and family and use its various features.

2. **https://www.assessmentday.co.uk/video-interviews. htm:** This is a free and simple place to practise. Once you reach the page, you can start the camera and recording. The page also has questions, which you can answer. This portal has features where you can play your recorded video or download it to watch later to evaluate and improve yourself.

12

Leaving a Job Gracefully

Breaking a relationship is always a tough emotional experience. You have reached a crossroads in your career, and it is time to let your boss know you are quitting your job. Whether you're leaving for a new position, launching your own business or taking time off, you need to know what to say when you quit your job in order to end things on a positive note. You are leaving the job, not the relationship you have built with people, including your office friends and boss. This severance is very likely to stir both you and your employer emotionally. It can be difficult to navigate this emotional turbulence. Still, you must move on gracefully—even if you hated your role, hated your boss, or are leaving a toxic work environment. You just have to keep moving forward on a positive note.

Sushil passed out from a reputed management college in 2018 and joined a top manufacturing company in Mumbai through a campus placement. He was happy with the company and the role, and everything was just a perfect start to his career. Manufacturing is a traditional set-up, with conventional designations and promotion policies. He became assistant manager after completing his stint as management trainee. He would be eligible for the next promotion after three years. He had been just two years in his job, when he learned that his batchmates from college who had joined new-age companies had been promoted to manager, and some even to senior manager. He started comparing his 'achievement' with theirs, and soon took a decision to leave the company. Since he was a good performer, his HR manager and a few senior leaders counselled him against it. They told him he was taking a wrong decision. Every company has its own designations, roles and HR policies; therefore, he should not compare himself with people from other industries but wait for his career to progress. He was assured that his aspirations would be taken care of. But he did not listen to anyone and left the company on a bad note. He spoiled his relationship with the people in his current company while leaving. He found a job in another good company at Ahmedabad as manager. He felt he had now caught up with his college mates.

But just six months into the job he realized that he had made an 'impulsive decision'. He started feeling that his previous company (and everything associated with it, like his role and designation there) was much better than his current company. He should not have left his previous job, he felt. He was desperate to change companies again. He approached his manager in the previous company and expressed his keenness to return. He sent his updated résumé for the same position he had had there earlier. The manager shared the profile with the HR manager, who consulted a few leaders in the company to seek their opinion on rehiring Sushil. Most said 'No'. Their reason for saying so was not Sushil's performance, but the manner in which he had quit the company, spoiling his relationship with everyone.

In current times, an employee generally remains at a company for only three or four years. Every company knows that employees will leave. It is natural, and happens in all companies. But *how* you leave is critical, as it has an impact on your professional relations. You should always keep some room for a subsequent return in the future to the company you are leaving. Always remember, 'rehiring' or 'boomerang hiring' is something that companies like to do. In fact, most companies have a formal 'rehiring policy', as their earlier employees already know the culture and values of the company and usually show increased loyalty and productivity after rejoining. The reasons for your leaving a company and the manner in which you left it are two critical factors the company considers when deciding whether you are worthy of rehiring or not.

A good departure has many benefits. Your relationship with your supervisors and co-workers will reinforce positive perceptions about your professionalism, and help you smoothly transition to the next phase of your career. It will also prevent you from burning any bridges, and keep the doors open for you in case you ever want to come back to your earlier company in the future. Don't forget, the professional world is small, and you may find your current boss and colleagues in your future places of employment too. Hence, it is always good to leave on a positive note.

Before You Break the News

Some bosses and companies are unpredictable. They may surprise you by releasing you the same day or cutting off your computer access on the same day. You may not have access to your computer, so it is advisable to store personal and important documents in advance.

- **Do clean up your computer by copying your work:** It is a given that everyone has some personal documents, pictures and other files stored on their official laptop, desktop or notebook, for practical reasons. Transfer them to your personal computer, personal email ID, Google Drive or online storage drive; also transfer some non-proprietary samples of your work and documents that will be helpful in future jobs. Forward important emails, awards, appreciation letters/certificates and other non-proprietary information to your personal email ID.

- **Make copies of personal documents, contacts and salary, and benefits-related details**: Please take both soft copies as well as printouts of personal documents (given below) which may be on the company's HR portal.

  o   Salary slips
  o   Annual compensation letter
  o   Increment letters
  o   Bonus letter
  o   PF statement
  o   Form 16 and income tax-related documents
  o   Compensation dues-related documents

o   Balance and accrued leave-related documents
o   Pension plans certificates
o   Company car, phone, laptop, or tablet-related documents
o   Other personal documents

Please also make a note of the contact information of key people and your colleagues in the company whom you would like to be in touch with.

How to Break the News of Your Resignation

Be mentally calm and professional in your approach. Some employers may take it positively, some may react badly— some may appreciate it, as it is part of professional life, and some may mistreat you or not appreciate you. Do not speak or write anything in haste. This will either come back to haunt you or destroy your peace of mind.

• **Meet your boss and key people to prepare:** Once you have received the offer letter in writing and have accepted the offer from your future employer, I would recommend that you first meet your boss and then the other key stakeholders. Do not tell them that you have decided to move on. Thank them, giving them reasons for your gratitude, and tell them that a very good opportunity has come your way, which you are exploring seriously. Also tell them that you will confirm the news in two or three days. This will act as a big trust-building factor for you. Keep your resignation letter and email ready, but wait for two or three days before sending them.

- **Meet key people personally, break the news with a gift and say thank you:** As mentioned earlier, the professional world is very small, and people you know will surely cross paths with you and influence your career at some point. You should not carry any heartburn against them. Try to live life light. You can't survive without developing relationships, especially in the corporate world. If you are in a job, you must try your best to keep things positive and not create any heartburn or spoil relationships while breaking the news of your leaving the company. In your mind, prepare a story of reasons to explain your departure to your manager. Whatever reasons you provide, keep your story consistent and keep your reasons positive, not negative.

Meet individually with mentors and sponsors within the company. Beyond your own department, if you have mentors or anyone within the company who has acted as your sponsor, you must meet them, share your story and tell them about your decision.

While there are many ways in which to resign from a company, the one I would recommend is the 'break the news with a gift' way. Everyone has emotions, and they need to be managed well for your long-lasting relationship with them. Use this time to communicate your appreciation for your boss and strengthen the relationship. If you have decided to move on, then make a list of key people (begin with your boss) with whom you want to share the news. However, it is important that you must know how to express your gratitude in the best possible manner. Expressing feelings is good, but presenting personalized gifts can appeal at an intimate level. Think about each of the persons you want to give something to, and make a list of the gifts that they may like. Buy a few gifts. At the same time, you need to be cautious in selecting your gifts, because the wrong gift can badly affect a relationship. Here are some of the items that you may consider for gifting:

- Notebook
- Digital calendar
- Inspiration board
- Personal sketch, poem, etc.
- Pen
- Digital photo frame
- Photo frame
- Leather planner

You must express your gratitude and convey your positive feelings along with the gift. *After your verbal conversation about your leaving, follow it up with your resignation letter/email.*

After you have personally met all the stakeholders and discussed with them your intention to resign, write a nice, professional and short formal resignation letter or email. Be full of praise for the company, the people, the culture . . . do not write anything negative in your resignation letter or email. Do not write your reasons for leaving the company, as different people may interpret them differently. You must include your personal phone number and email ID so that people who want to stay connected with you can get in touch with you.

A sample resignation letter or email:

Subject: [your name] Resignation
Dear Mr/Ms [Name of your manager],

I thank you for your time today and I appreciate your guidance and mentorship once again. Working with my colleagues, the leadership team and everyone at [name of the company] was an honour and a privilege, which I will cherish for life and take with me into the next chapter of my life. It is very hard for me to say goodbye.

As discussed with you today, I am resigning as [your designation or role] with effect from today. Please accept my resignation and confirm my release date. As per the terms of my appointment, my notice period is three months. I will be fully committed to executing my responsibilities and handing them over to the person you nominate during this time.

The last three years that I have worked here have been the most fruitful years of my life and have helped me grow both professionally and personally. I have enjoyed my tenure here. I appreciate the support, guidance and encouragement you have provided me. My experience here and my relationship with my colleagues have made a world of difference in my life.

I would appreciate your continued advice and mentorship as I start the next phase of my career.

I can be reached at my personal email address [personal email ID] or cell phone [mobile number].

Thanks again for your support and guidance.

Best regards,

[Your name]

[Email ID]

[Mobile number]

[Social media accounts for connecting]

Things to Do after Resigning

There are three things that can happen during the meeting with your boss:

a. Your boss can accept your resignation.
b. Your boss can ask what they can do to make you stay and try to retain you.
c. Your boss can react poorly to your decision to leave.

In the case of the first two options, you should thank your boss and other seniors. If you trust them, you can be open with them and tell them about your new role, compensation and other benefits, which led you to decide to quit. They may offer insights, which may help you. They may also offer you some advice relating to your new role, location or compensation, or address some of your current concerns. That would be helpful, especially if you are in an early stage of your professional career. Some decide to quit in a hurry, and such insights from a senior may help you reflect on things in totality and guide you to make an informed decision.

Since you have decided to resign, keep all aspects in mind before breaking the news to them. It is advisable not to change your decision and get retained by the company. However, if you trust your bosses and like the company, there is no harm in staying back too, especially if you realize that your decision is not right.

- **Be positive and speak positive:** Always remember, the reason for your next job is the current job. Always emphasize the positive and talk about how the company has benefited you, even though it's time to move on. There's no point in being negative.

- **Be humble and do not talk too much about the new job:** Even if you have just got the best job in the world, be humble and do not talk too much about it. Doing that and bragging about it anyway does not matter to your current colleagues and is not going to help you in any way.

- **Connect with colleagues on social media, write recommendations for them and request them to write some for you:** If you are already connected on social media, write a few LinkedIn recommendations for your supervisors and colleagues. People love receiving recommendations, and it will help you get some for yourself too. You can also request supervisors, customers, subordinates, suppliers and colleagues to write recommendations for you.

If your boss reacts badly to your decision, keep your calm. Understand that as long as you have delivered the news politely and professionally, your boss's reaction is not in your control. What is in your control is your decision to respond or not. Appreciate the fact that your boss may have groomed you and taken pains to train you. His reaction, therefore, is natural. Listen to him and appreciate him. Go to him after some time when he is in a good mood and do two things:

Thank him. Express your gratitude for the opportunity you got to grow in your current job and learn new skills. Say thank you for the chance to work with him and the team.

An offer to help during the transition. Give him confidence that you will do your best and ensure complete knowledge transfer, help train a replacement and/or also be available to answer questions after you have moved on.

Dealing with the Fallout

Even if you've worked for the company for a long time, you can't predict what will happen when you resign. Your manager may ask you to leave immediately, or to stay longer, or to reconsider your decision entirely. The best way to deal with this uncertainty is to prepare for every possibility.

- **Have a plan for the following outcomes, and you won't be caught off guard:**
  - **Be prepared to leave immediately:** As advised earlier also, be sure to back up any documents and projects belonging to you. Understand that your employer

might ask you to pack up your things immediately and may cut off electronic access to documents.

Take the time to write a personal email or note to the colleagues who've supported you and whom you would like to keep in touch with.

Key Takeaways

1. The reason for your next job is your current job. Be positive, give and carry good memories.
2. Take a back-up of all personal documents, employment records, before breaking the news.
3. Be personal, positive and grateful while breaking the news.
4. Prepare yourself for a range of different reactions to your resignation.
5. Thank everyone and stay connected with key people at the company.

Exercise

1. Prepare your reasons for your resignation and make sure the story is consistent.
2. Make a list of key seniors and peers whom you want to personally thank.
3. Thank them with a gift and move out on a positive note.